CAULDRON
OF
MEMORY

Michael Tyler

About the Author

Raven Grimassi is a Neo-Pagan scholar and award-winning author of more than a dozen books on Witchcraft, Wicca, and Neo-Paganism. He is a member of the American Folklore Society and is co-founder and co-director of the College of the Crossroads.

Raven's background includes training in the Rosicrucian Order as well as the study of the Kabbalah through the First Temple of Tifareth under Lady Sara Cunningham. His early magical career began in the late 1960s and involved the study of works by Franz Bardon, Eliphas Levi, William Barrett, Dion Fortune, William Gray, William Butler, and Israel Regardie.

Today, Raven is the directing Elder of the tradition of Arician Witchcraft, and together with his wife, Stephanie Taylor, he is developing a complete teaching system known as Ash, Birch, and Willow. This system is the culmination of over thirty-five years of study and practice in the magical and spiritual traditions of the indigenous people of pre-Christian Europe.

Retrieving Ancestral
Knowledge & Wisdom

CAULDRON
OF
MEMORY

RAVEN
GRIMASSI

Llewellyn Publications
Woodbury, Minnesota

First Edition
First Printing, 2009

Cover art © 2009 Linda Joyce Franks
Cover design by Lisa Novak
Editing by Connie Hill
Interior illustrations on pages 21–22, 61, 103, 111, 114, 130, 145, 172, 174, 176–179, 193, and 197 © 2009 Carol Coogan. All other interior art by Llewellyn Art department.
Cards on pages 84, 88, 90, 92, 116 and 120 from *The Hidden Path* by Raven Grimassi and Stephanie Taylor, art work by Mickie Mueller, reprinted with permission.
Cards on pages 82, 79, 98, 118, 122, and 142 from *The Well Worn Path* by Raven Grimassi and Stephanie Taylor, art work by Mickie Mueller, reprinted with permission.
Llewellyn is a registered trademark of Llewellyn Worldwide, Ltd.

Library of Congress Cataloging-in-Publication Data)
Grimassi, Raven, 1951–
  Cauldron of memory : retrieving ancestral knowledge & wisdom / by
Raven Grimassi. — 1st ed.
     p.   cm.
  Includes bibliographical references and index.
  ISBN 978-0-7387-1575-9
  1. Occultism. 2. Spirituality. 3. Memory—Miscellanea. 4. Morphogenesis—
Miscellanea. 5. Consciousness—Miscellanea. 6. Resonance—Miscellanea.
I. Title.
  BF1999.G79   2009
  130—dc22   2009022058

Llewellyn Worldwide does not participate in, endorse, or have any authority or responsibility concerning private business transactions between our authors and the public.

All mail addressed to the author is forwarded but the publisher cannot, unless specifically instructed by the author, give out an address or phone number.

Any Internet references contained in this work are current at publication time, but the publisher cannot guarantee that a specific location will continue to be maintained. Please refer to the publisher's website for links to authors' websites and other sources.

The publisher does not endorse or recommend the use of the participant's blood in ritual practices.

Llewellyn Publications
A Division of Llewellyn Worldwide, Ltd.
2143 Wooddale Drive, Dept. 978-0-7387-1575-9
Woodbury, Minnesota 55125-2989, U.S.A.
www.llewellyn.com

Printed in the United States of America

Other Books by Raven Grimassi

Beltane: Springtime Rituals, Lore & Celebration

Crafting Wiccan Traditions

Encyclopedia of Wicca & Witchcraft

Hereditary Witchcraft: Secrets of the Old Religion

Italian Witchcraft: The Old Religion of Southern Europe

Spirit of the Witch: Religion & Spirituality in Contemporary Witchcraft

The Wiccan Mysteries: Ancient Origins & Teachings

Wiccan Magick: Inner Teachings of the Craft

Witchcraft: A Mystery Tradition

The Witches' Craft: The Roots of Witchcraft & Magical Transformation

The Witch's Familiar: Spiritual Partnerships for Successful Magic

The Hidden Path
with Stephanie Taylor and Mickie Mueller

The Well Worn Path
with Stephanie Taylor and Mickie Mueller

Acknowledgments

I wish to acknowledge my friend, fellow author, and teacher, R. J. Stewart. Over the past decade I have participated in his workshops and have passed time with him in personal conversation. His work with mystical cords and inner planes contacts has been very inspirational to this book. It is with great admiration and appreciation that I acknowledge this remarkable practitioner and teacher.

Contents

PREFACE

This book is about things that are both ancient and contemporary at the same time. In order to avoid any misunderstanding of the material in this book, or any misinterpretation of my reasons for writing it, I want to state at the outset that I created this system myself. I did not, however, create the components that make up this system.

For the purposes of this book, when I speak of "ancient" I am talking about tenets that are rooted in antiquity. In other words, the concepts in this book originate from ancestral beliefs and practices. My presentation here is my personal interpretation and expression. I am not claiming that the system I present is traceable as a whole to any specific religious, ritual, or magical system of which we have any record.

Throughout this book I will be sharing what I call the cauldron system. Its primary function is to retrieve ancestral knowledge, which I believe resides in our DNA. I regard this knowledge as a type of inner communication that our ancestors called the ancestral spirit.

My approach to gathering and constructing the cauldron system is to use elements that appear in old tales as connections to mystical themes. These themes, in turn, connect with the magical view of our ancestors. We can then trace the ancestral view to its source. This is what I call the memory-chain associations, which is what shamans might call the ivy vine that moves through the inner worlds.

In this book I also draw upon a relatively new field of science known as morphogenetics. This is an approach through biology to attempt to explain the process of evolution and various types of phenomena that appear in the "knowledge" of many life forms, which to date have been viewed as unintelligent reactions to chemical processes.

Underlying the chapters is the theme of two types of reality: material reality and nonmaterial reality. It is my belief that we are spiritual beings temporarily encased in material bodies, and therefore we operate with two corresponding levels of consciousness. One part of our consciousness is designed to function within the requirements of our material condition. The other half is intended to see inner meaning and discern the lessons that physical life can teach.

To apply this concept to the material in the book, I have drawn upon spiritual and magical traditions that involve the use of a physical tool. This tool is the cauldron, and I explore old myths, legends, and lore about cauldrons as metaphors for the work of the cauldron system.

As discussed in this book, I view the ancient Bard as a prophet who left messages for future generations. These messages were intended for those who would one day live in a world whose soul they have forgotten. The Bard spoke for the *disconnected* who no longer honor the earth as the Mother, and who therefore find themselves lost. For such a time, the Bard wrote stories of the lost cauldron and the need to engage on a Quest of retrieval.

This book speaks to what we have collectively lost as a modern people. Its purpose is to provide a vision and call us to the Quest of regeneration and renewal (the attributes ascribed to the mystical cauldrons themselves). Beyond that, this book is a message and a reminder, a call to reclaim the personal power that others do not want you to know you possess. The spiritual map for this quest is found in the chapters that await you.

INTRODUCTION

Several years ago I undertook some training in a folkloric system of what has come to be known as the Faery tradition. Through this work, I later encountered what I believe to be Faery beings operating as a group known as the Lantra. They profess to be the keepers and bearers of a mystical light that is connected to the inner mystery tradition of the Underworld forces.

Part of my training included author R. J. Stewart's work with the application of ritual or magical cords. Such cords appear in many traditions and have a variety of uses. In my own personal tradition of Italian witchcraft, we find the use of three colored cords: black, red, and white. These are used for spellcasting, ritual work, and spiritual practice. However, the use of cords as taught by R. J. Stewart is much more involved than the system known to me in my private practice of Italian witchcraft.

For the purposes of this book, and the system it presents, I have joined together various elements of the Faery tradition with my own system. In the early stages of creating this system I was quite surprised to encounter the god Hermes within the mechanism. I previously knew little about Hermes and mistakenly regarded him in very simplistic ways. This was quickly corrected when I came to realize the great depth and antiquity at the core of this remarkable deity form. In the end Hermes took on an important role in the system now presented in this book.

As you will discover in the forthcoming chapters, the inner mechanisms of pathworking and inner planes connections are essential to working with this system. Altered states of consciousness have always been part of inner mystery traditions and shamanic work. The latter has particular appeal for many people and is an important component in this book.

During my research, I encountered several texts that dealt with anthropological investigations and experimentations connected with South American tribes and the use of mind-altering drugs. I also reflected back on the work of Carlos Castaneda, who wrote on Mesoamerica shamanism. However, I did not draw upon this as a resource while writing my book, as his material is highly controversial and its authenticity is questioned by many, but as a practicing occultist for over thirty years, I do recognize authentic traditional elements in Castaneda's work regarding the depiction of techniques and metaphysical concepts.

In shamanic practice we typically find the presence of serpents in one form or another. Serpents also frequently appear in traditions that incorporate ancestral veneration. In many myths and legends, the serpent is a messenger between the realm of the dead and the world of the living. For this reason I have included the serpent as a spirit-form and an ally within the operational aspects of the inner system presented in the book.

Within the structure of the presented system I have incorporated the Faery ally. Although the basic concept of Faery companions does appear within Italian witchcraft, I have also added material influenced through what I was taught by R. J. Stewart. However, it should be noted that what I present here is much simpler in scope and is my own design.

I do not wish to leave the impression that the material in this book is specifically Italian or southern European in nature. It actually reflects very old views that are also common to other regions of Europe and the British Isles. Therefore, the system is intended for use by people with a diversity of cultural interests.

Among the oldest mystery systems we find that of the Underworld tradition. Its connection with ancestral spirits is obvious, but the importance of this tradition also lies in its inherent forces related to life, death, and rebirth. One of the core elements of the system presented in this book is that of ancestral contact and communication. As you will discover, there are various levels and factors that define what is meant by communication with the ancestors.

There are many stories associated with the Underworld that include a mystical cauldron. In such tales, the cauldron is at the heart of the Underworld and possesses mystical properties and powers. Cauldron stories reflect an inner process, a brewing and distilling of elements that ultimately produce something singular and profound. In keeping with this theme, I present a series of stages to take you through an inner process of internal communication. But as with all things of a mystical nature, the inner leads to the outer and vice versa. You will find that the microcosm and the macrocosm meet in the inner cauldron.

In the chapters ahead, you will discover a variety of shamanic tools. These include a simple stone that represents the sacred land, a wand with ribbons used to unravel the mysteries, and a special tool known as the Sacred Tree. The Sacred Tree is a configuration of three cords united as one, which is used for inner planes journeys (a type of shaman's ladder) and for memory retrieval.

The tools described in this book are easy to make and can be constructed of readily available materials. Ritual and magical tools are an integral part of many mystery traditions and are useful aids. Over the course of time you will no doubt learn other uses and techniques for these tools on your own. However, in the beginning, I encourage you to work with the tools as instructed until such time as you feel comfortable experimenting on your own. It may be that you will end up not using one of the tools and replacing it with something of your own.

In the last half of this book you will find several chapters involving ancestral spirits and methods of veneration. Maintaining an active connection with your spiritual lineage is key to the work presented in this book. Through your inner cauldron the past, present, and future join together in one meeting place.

The final element of the system presented in this book is rooted in the new biological science of metamorpho-genetic fields. The theory of metamorphics attempts to explain non-audio communication between living organisms. This involves generated energy fields that serve as a catalyst for change and awareness.

An important aspect of metamorphic fields is the theory of resonance. This involves the idea that energy fields create a vibration or wave that travels through time. This resonance carries with it the imbedded thoughts and actions of its creators in the form of energy patterns. The principle of metamorphic resonance is similar to the echo effect of sound. But in the case of a metamorphic field there is no deterioration or cessation of the travelling wave.

Communication through inner and outer levels is at the center of this book. We all exist in a web of interlaced energy patterns that connect all things together. This web contains the past, present, and future—all of which exist simultaneously. In this light, "time" exists only as a fleeting moment of awareness, as our consciousness rises and submerges amidst the waves of morphogenetic resonance.

Through the techniques in this book you can become aware of both internal and external levels of communication. This can offer you access to transformational forces and help integrate aspects of your consciousness that can work together for greater productivity. In the pages of this book you will find a spiritual map leading you to the core of your own personal power. The quest awaits you.

ONE

IN SEARCH OF THE CAULDRON

Does a particular period of history fascinate you? Do you sometimes wish you could go back in time and talk with your ancestors? If you could travel back in time, what questions would you ask? Why would you want to know the answers in the first place?

As modern people, we tend to think that time moves from the present, flowing on its way into the future. Because of this we tend to think of the past as something that no longer exists. But what if *time* isn't like a flowing river, but instead is like a lake? In this analogy, time is like the water in the lake; it is everywhere at once. If this is truly the case, then we can move from one area to another and, in effect, visit the past and the future simply by shifting our present location.

One popular image of time travel is the time machine. In science fiction stories, such a machine can take you to any time period you wish to visit. It can also return you back to where you began. Time travel stories are always about leaving the present. But what if time travel is possible, and instead of traveling backward it actually involves bringing the past into the present? In this light, "shifting our present location" means altering our consciousness. Here we are not leaving the present; we are joining it with the past.

In the course of this book you will be offered a way to connect with the past. I am not talking about making a time machine. Instead I will demonstrate that your mind, body, and spirit can operate as a type of time machine. However, you will not be journeying through time dimensions—you will be traveling to an inner place where all time periods meet. This place is associated with your DNA, which contains a set of genetic instructions from the *past* that are given to you in the *present* with the intention of creating a *future*. This means that you are already the living center of all time periods meeting together as one.

The primary purpose of this book is to teach several foundational techniques through which you can retrieve information from the past. Through the exercises in this book you can tap into ancestral memory. There is much wisdom and knowledge to be gained from such a venture.

If you think about it on a mundane level, you are currently the culmination of all your experiences. This includes everything from the day you were born until this very moment in which you are reading this book. All of your strengths, character, knowledge, and wisdom exist because of your past experiences. Now imagine joining this with the culmination of each of these same qualities possessed by all of your ancestors. If you could do this *consciously*, then it would be incredibly powerful and enlightening. You would experience yourself as a much greater being than you are aware of at present.

We've read about great heroes from ancient times. What set them apart from the average person was their experiences. They possessed an inner quality that made them people of great renown. One clue to this quality is found in the stories about them. At the center of such stories is the idea of a quest. The quest is always about obtaining something that is considered lost or hidden. At the end of the story this item is retrieved and it bestows its gift of transformation. This is what makes the character legendary. It is all about integration and wholeness, becoming more than you were when you first set out.

The theme of a quest and transformation appears profoundly in the ancient tales of a mystical or magical cauldron. Throughout the book we will work with this theme as a metaphor for an inward journey of enlightenment and personal transformation. In various chapters you will discover useful tools that can be easily constructed to help you along the way.

The ultimate goal of this book is to teach you how to find an inner place that I call the *Cauldron of Memory*. This is, in effect, a journey down to the cellular levels of your being. It is where the living memory of your lineage flows from the hidden messages residing in your DNA. This is where the ancestral spirit lives and breathes.

In the chapters ahead, you will find several techniques using three centers of power within your body. These are symbolized as three inner cauldrons. Each of the cauldron exercises incorporates visualizations that activate the associated power centers. Not only can these centers be used for retrieving ancestral memory, these inner cauldrons can *brew* energy for healing and for magical work. They can also enhance your rituals through the generation of altered states of consciousness. This is all fully described in other chapters.

In ancient myth and legend, journeys are always required in order for significant changes to take place. No one gets anywhere by remaining where they are in any of the old tales. Ahead in several chapters you will be guided through a series of inner journeys using images and a storyline. This technique is known as pathworking. Until sometime around the mid-1980s, this was a method of training almost entirely unknown outside of old occult societies.

Pathworking is a journey of the mind between what is known in the material world and what is unknown in the non-material realms. This system uses creative imagination, but this kind of imagination is not the fanciful type of daydreams or popular games requiring visualization. In pathworking, imagination is the use of images that move the consciousness into inner planes of reality. Images become the vehicles that carry our consciousness into other worlds.

Later in this book you will encounter several pathwork exercises. They are designed to allow you access into hidden realms that will lead you to the Cauldron of Memory. Every pathwork contains a doorway or portal of some type, which opens into another realm. These realms (or their essential components) have been preserved in ancient stories.

It is well known among the inner mystery traditions that old myths and legends contain the secret of the way into the worlds they describe. This is missed only by those who regard the old tales as mere stories of entertainment or moral value. It is the deeper levels of these stories that contain the hidden elements of an esoteric nature.

In the pages of this book you will work with some important esoteric themes. They will be introduced in other chapters, but a few words about them should be said at this time. One of the central or core themes is that of the portal. Entrances into other worlds are most often represented by doors or gates. A symbol or sign on the door points to a particular realm that waits behind the doorway. Sometimes the portal is a place such as a crossroads.

The place of the crossroads is sometimes known as a spirit gate. This is due to the ancient legends that souls of the dead gathered at the crossroads. One important deity associated with the crossroads is the god Hermes. He was a god of roads and pathways, as well as an escort of the dead. In some tales he also aids in the return of souls to the mortal world.

The souls of the dead were under the care of Hermes as they traveled the road between the world of the living and the realm of the dead. He protected these souls as well as all travelers of any kind. From this attribute arose the belief that images of Hermes at the crossroads had the power to avert evil on any road or journey. As a god of the roads, he was immune from the associated perils of the way, and bestowed this immunity upon anyone who invoked his aid.

As previously mentioned, later in this book you will be performing several pathworkings. These will take your consciousness on a journey to other realms of nonmaterial existence. Therefore we will be calling upon the aid of Hermes to ensure positive outcomes from our travels as we pass through the boundaries that separate the planes. Hermes is a valuable companion who aids us as we pass from the familiar into the unknown.

The name Hermes is derived from a term used to denote a heap of stones marking a boundary or crossroad. From this basic concept Hermes evolved into a god of boundaries or crossroads, both physical and psychological. In this regard Hermes represents "the in-between" places, and he possesses the ability to join and balance multiple levels of meaning, which renders him the connection-maker.

In addition to representing the boundary or crossroad, Hermes also signifies the ability to effect transition and transformation. Therefore, for the purposes of our work to come in this book, Hermes is a key character. He can aid us in crossing boundaries and returning. Hermes can also help us to balance multiple levels of consciousness. This is important to our work as we develop the inner levels of our being through pathworking.

In ancient writings (one example is Homer's Hymn to Hermes), Hermes is described as a god who is particularly friendly to humans and loves to companion them. He protected heralds as they traveled on the roads, and through this connection he became linked to messengers and messages from all over the known world. As a result, he eventually took on the role of interpreting anything foreign. This was most likely due to his knowledge of the known and the unknown through his widespread travels. Later we will draw upon his aid in interpreting ancestral memories retrieved through techniques in this book.

Hermes is sometimes called "the wall-piercer" due to ancient writings that ascribe to him the ability to glide edgeways through the keyhole of a building like wind or mist. This magical nature possessed by Hermes is found in many Otherworld beings of myth and legend throughout Europe; likewise the very nature of Hermes appears in the gods of northern Europe. Therefore it is not surprising to find that Hermes has been equated with various Celtic and Germanic gods.

In the book *Britannia After the Romans,* by Algernon Herbert (1836, p. 66), the author equates Hermes with the legendry Celtic figure known as Gwion (who becomes the bard, Taliesin). The author writes:

> [Gwion] *appears to be the Hermes or Mercury whom the ancient Britons revered above all other deities, and who (in the alchemic superstitions) presided over the permutations of nature. The circumstance, that Gwion's name has no assignable etymology, is much in favour of its high antiquity. Hermes is more usually styled in the Neo-British jargon Gwydion ap Don, preserver of men, artificer of the rainbow, sublime astrologer, exorcist of evil spirits, and inventor of the hierographic alphabet. The death of Aeddon of Mona is termed his departure from*

the Land of Gwydion into the ark, which latter is a Bardic symbol of the grave. Gwlad-Wydion is therefore either Britannia in general or Mona. Before the Romans came, our island was the supreme and appellate seat of the Druidical orgies and doctrine. That sect worshipped the god Mercury above all others, of him they had the most numerous idols, they celebrated him as the inventor of all arts, and they considered him as their guide in all voyages or journeys, and as having the greatest influence over commerce and pecuniary gain. Of all his forms and attributes, that of Mercury, the Merchant, was the most reverenced throughout Celtica. His idol carried a large bag in its hand, and his Gallic inscriptions ran Mercuric Negotiatori and Mercurio Nundinatori; while, in the barbarous Latin of the Cymmry, Mercurius Mercator (or mercedis auctor) could barely recognize himself as Marca Mercedus. In the circumstance of carrying a bag, the Celtic Mercury seems to agree with Gwion, for the latter was termed Gwion Gwd, i.e. Gwion of the Bag.

In the book Iron and Steel in Ancient Times (2005), author Vagn Buchwald mentions an ancient Etruscan mirror that bears an engraving of Hermes with a cauldron in his hands (circa 400 BCE). This item is in Thorvaldsen's Museum in Copenhagen. Ancient myths describe Hermes restoring life to the legendary figure, known as Pelops, by placing him in a cauldron. The theme of a cauldron of regeneration is an important one to the premise of this book, for it connects with the role of DNA.

In the next chapter we will explore the idea of the cauldron of regeneration. In addition we will take note of other mystical cauldrons. Through these concepts the connection will be made to an inner Cauldron of Memory, which brews the mystical essence of what has been passed to us through our DNA. Let us move to the next chapter and begin our journey to find the hidden cauldron.

TWO

THE CAULDRON OF REGENERATION

Throughout the course of this book we will look at themes associated with cauldrons, but this is not meant to be a book about cauldrons or cauldron lore, per se. The intent of this book is to reveal an inner spiritual tradition that can be as real and alive for you as it was for your pagan ancestors. It is a book about restoring and implementing something you may never have known was lost. However, you may very likely feel that *something* is missing but you can't quite put your finger on exactly what this might be.

The thing your spirit ultimately longs for already resides within you, but unfortunately mundane life may have placed brambles in the way or created endless detours around the peace, contentment, and happiness you seek most. The good news is that a spiritual map already exists that can bypass these barriers. The way was once well known but has been neglected over the centuries. Fortunately our ancestors preserved this travel guide for us in the form of stories about the quest for the lost or hidden cauldron. Therefore, to truly benefit you need to understand the foundational elements of cauldron myth and legend.

Myths and legends about cauldrons are extremely ancient. In such tales the cauldron is depicted as a mystical or magical vessel. These vessels are connected to themes that include abundance, enlightenment, replenishment, and regeneration. The latter is our primary focus throughout this book, but we will also explore the cauldron theme as it pertains to enlightenment. We all desire to be enlightened beings, have abundance in our lives, and be able to replenish our resources. The cauldron legends hold valuable clues for us in this quest.

An examination of the legends associated with the Cauldron of Regeneration reveals that this vessel symbolizes the womb of the Mother Goddess, the earth itself. It is intimately connected with water (and other fluids) as well as with the Underworld or Otherworld of myth and legend. Both of these mystical realms are associated with bodies of water. In many tales of the Underworld, we find descriptions of rivers. Legends of the Otherworld tell us of a great island in a lake, or of a far-off kingdom beyond the western horizon of the sea. In metaphysical philosophy water is often associated with our psyche and our emotions.

In *The Mythology and Rites of the Druids* (1809) by Edward Davies, the legendary figure known as Ceridwen is depicted as a mother goddess and is associated with the sea. Davies states that Ceridwen presides in a floating island sanctuary and is the "proprietor of the mystic cauldron" that originates from Hu, the "emperor" of the sea. Davies identifies Ceridwen with a boat (the sacred ark) that traverses the waters, and also with the moon above. Such vessels are often associated with the journey of the soul and serve as a conveyor. In one ancient belief, we find that departed souls traveled to the moon and were later reincarnated on the earth.

In most legends, Ceridwen's cauldron bestows the gift of poetic inspiration as well as the enlightenment required to unravel and understand all mysteries. Davies states that this cauldron was attended by nine maidens in a four-cornered castle sanctuary within the sacred island. He refers to them as *"the Gwyllion, certain prophetesses of mythology, who gave the first presage of the deluge, by their nightly songs, in the bosoms of lakes; that is, in their sacred islands."* Gwyllion, the name of these maidens, is the plural of Gwyll, which in old lore is a night wanderer, a fairy, or a witch. The Gwyll are often called the *children of the evening.* This is reflective of the guiding inner voice we hear in times of discernment, questioning, and judgment.

In the most popular tale, Ceridwen's cauldron created a special brew so powerful that only three drops were enough to bestow genius on a mortal man. The liquid in the cauldron required "a year and a day" to brew. In Celtic lore the phrase "a year and a day" refers to a cycle of completion as well as to formal initiation. The latter is at the core of Ceridwen's brew, which ultimately results in the transformation and rebirth of the famous bard known as Taliesin. It is here that we understand our inherent power to become whatever we envision for ourselves.

The theme of transformation is essential to our understanding of the cauldron mysteries. As you read the other chapters of this book, you will discover something important. Many of the key elements contained in cauldron lore also pertain to essential things hidden within your material body, your psyche, and soul or spirit. These correspondences will become clear as you move through the chapters.

Transformation is always the active force in tales of the Cauldron of Regeneration. One example is found in the legend of Bran, which comes from the classic work known as the Mabinogion. One legend tells us that Bran became the possessor of a magical cauldron. Upon receiving it, Bran is informed that if a dead warrior is placed inside the cauldron, by morning he will leave the cauldron alive and at his best. However, the warrior will not be able to regain his speech.

Bran's cauldron was brought from the Lake of the Cauldron near a sacred mound in Ireland. In northern European tradition, we often find that mounds are portals to the Faery world. Once accessed, these mounds open to reveal a descending stone staircase. According to legend, the stairs lead into a cavern through which access to the Faery Realm is granted. Old ballads refer to Otherworld features and many mystical elements in the Faery Realm are associated with the souls of the dead who must pass through this land on their way to the Underworld. This typically involves traversing a great lake or some other body of water. Reaching the other side involves a boat, a bridge, or a set of stepping stones (or leaping stones). There is an important pattern here, and we will explore it further in forthcoming chapters.

As previously mentioned, the dead who are restored to life in Bran's cauldron cannot speak. It is noteworthy that in tales of the Underworld by the ancient Greek writer, Homer, the dead are mute until they are given some drops of blood by the living. It is the memory of the blood that restores speech. In the case of reincarnation, the ability to remember past lives can be overshadowed and the inner voice is mute. Like the warriors in Bran's cauldron, we are alive again but cannot speak (of our former life). Therefore we must taste the blood of our ancestors, which resides deep within the ancestral Cauldron of Memory.

One of the primary goals of this book is to help you envision yourself as the ancestral cauldron. Your blood is the magical brew and your DNA is the mystical inner force of transformation. You are, in effect, the living Cauldron of Memory. The exercises and alignments that follow will help you understand why this is important and what you can achieve through the system offered in this book. But before we move on to the practical work, it will be beneficial to look deeper into the cauldron mysteries.

The Cauldron Mysteries

Cauldrons play a principal role in myths and legends associated with the inner mysteries. The cauldron appears in the lore of all regions of Europe from Britain to the Mediterranean. It is in Celtic tradition that the theme of the lost or hidden cauldron uniquely appears (as though this theme represents something just out of reach within the Celtic psyche).

Almost without exception, Celtic cauldron myths are tales of sacred quests and the personal transformation that results from the journey. The cauldron is always located in the dungeon of a distant mysterious castle, the Land of the Dead, or a secret realm within the Otherworld of Celtic lore. The hero must journey and brave many encounters before reaching the cauldron and obtaining what it holds. No matter what the cauldron contains in such tales, the prize is always one of transformation. Transformations of all kinds are an integral part of Celtic mythology.

Over time, with the rise of Christianity, the old tales of pagan heroes were displaced with a Christian mythos. One example is the tale of the Arthurian quest for the Holy Grail. Here the ancient lunar cauldron of the goddess appears to be transformed into the chalice used by Christ at the Last Supper. Very little of its mystical symbolism seems changed however, and it is still a symbol of enlightenment and spiritual transformation. The tales of the Celtic bard, Taliesin, contain many elements that are part of the Arthurian quest mythos.

In Taliesin's poem "The Spoils of Annwn," a group of adventurers descend into the mystical realm of Annwn to recover the missing cauldron. In one story it is located in Caer Sidi or Caer Pedryan, the four-cornered castle, which is also known as Castle Spiral. As a symbol, the spiral was used in tomb decoration to represent death and renewal. It is here in the center of the spiral (itself within the center of the castle) that the adventurers discover the Cauldron of Ceridwen.

The tale of the descent into Annwn is representative of many mystery teachings. One aspect concerns itself with the lunar mysteries. Here the missing cauldron of Ceridwen represents the waning of the moon and its disappearance for three days (prior to the return of the crescent in the night sky). For the ancients, the moon's absence was a time of dread. Therefore the moon must be retrieved from the Underworld into which it seemingly descends each night. The quest to retrieve the cauldron of Ceridwen is, in part, a quest to retrieve the sacred light of the moon. The Cauldron is the source of that light and therefore belongs to the Goddess. It is where enlightenment dwells in the center of darkness (just as solutions arise from conflicts).

In myth and legend, the cauldron brews certain potions, aids in the casting of spells, produces abundance or decline, and is a holy vessel for offerings to the powers of the night, and to the Great Goddess. As previously noted, its main attribute is that of transformation, whether of a spiritual or physical nature. As a symbol of the Goddess it can bestow wisdom, knowledge, and inspiration. This is symbolized by the light of the moon, itself represented by the glowing embers beneath the enchanted cauldron.

In the tale of the Cauldron of Ceridwen, the basic story recounts how Ceridwen prepared a brew in her cauldron designed to impart enlightenment to her son. The brew is accidentally tasted by Gwion, whose task it was to tend the cauldron. This act angers Ceridwen and she pursues Gwion as he tries to escape her wrath. This leads to a series of transformations as both characters shapeshift into various occult animals during the chase.

The mystical brew at the heart of this story reportedly consisted of yellow flowers known as the Pipes of Lleu (cowslip), Gwion's silver (fluxwort), the borues of Gwion (hedge-berry), Taliesin's cresses (vervain), and mistletoe berries mixed with sea foam. The dredge of this brew was reportedly extremely poisonous and required special handling.

A similar brew appears in ancient Greek tradition where it is created in the cauldron of Ceres. Its residue was likewise a poisonous substance made of herbal ingredients mixed with sea water. This theme, at its core, is connected to important inner teachings found in the blood mysteries.

In the advanced levels of the ancient mystery traditions, a potentially deadly potion was prepared for the willing initiate whereby he or she could retrieve genetic ancestral memories through an altered state of consciousness. Because the poison generates a near-death experience our inner survival mechanisms engage to tap into the cumulative knowledge of our genetic material in search of instructions on how to escape impending death. Surviving this experience ultimately resulted in a conscious merging with the *atavistic* collective consciousness/subconsciousness of our ancestors as retained in our DNA (the cauldron hidden in the Underworld). Support for this concept appears to be reflected in a comment made by scientist Carl Sagan in his book *Shadows of Forgotten Ancestors* (1992). Sagan remarks that our DNA possesses unknown elements that may be "survival keys" that once served our ancestors.

For us as a modern people, the idea of participating in such an intense and dangerous initiatory experience can be a shocking deterrent. The good news is that you do not have to try, and I strongly advise that you don't experiment with dangerous things of this nature. The reason you don't have to engage in these old methods is because the work has already been done and the way is already paved. It's recorded in your DNA. Because of your ancestors you now walk on the well-worn path.

In occult teachings, we encounter two important concepts: *inner planes contacts* and *memory-chain associations*. The inner contacts are sometimes called allies, guides, or co-walkers. These are beings that have already achieved the level of consciousness and personal transformation that are part of the Cauldron Quest mentality and spirituality. Part of their work is to assist and guide incarnate souls in the material realm. When you begin working with the Cauldron of Memory you will attract these beings, and if you work with them they can be of great help on your spiritual path.

Memory-chain associations are pre-formed patterns that exist as cohesive forms of energy within the earth's atmosphere and within the astral dimension. They react in much the same way as a row of dominos do when triggered to fall in an extended line. By analogy, each domino is an ancestral memory that formed due to its intensity (whether this was a ritual practice, a powerful shamanic technique, or what have you). Once you align yourself with something that is aligned with another thing, then you begin to tip the connective dominos. Unlike the domino effect, however, working with ancestral memory returns the wave of energy back to you. When it returns it carries the memory of where it has been and what it encountered.

If you think this all sounds very fanciful, then you are in for a surprise. There are actually aspects of biology and physics that support the basic mechanism of these principles. New discoveries in these fields are leading us to the realization that many occult and metaphysical sciences are based in the way things actually work (as opposed to old, worn-out models that science has relied upon for many decades).

In the following chapters, you will be introduced to several new concepts. Some of these are mixed with traditional teachings and some blaze new trails. Even though we walk the well-worn path of our ancestors we will ultimately arrive in unexplored territory. It then falls to us to be the ones to extend the path further for those who follow behind us. The sacred quest lies ahead.

THREE

THE INNER TRADITION

Today we hear a great deal about traditions. Some people speak of old traditions, eclectic systems, or self-styled traditions. There is however another lesser-known form of tradition. This is the "inner tradition," or esoteric system. It is also one of the most misunderstood traditions for a variety of reasons. In this book I hope to help increase the understanding of what an inner tradition is, and why it is important.

For the purposes of this book, when we talk about inner traditions, we need to share the same understanding in order to avoid confusion. So just what is an inner tradition? The short answer is that it's a system based upon an agreement of consciousness between members of the tradition. In other words, an inner tradition exists and functions within the group mind of the people that sustain it.

One example of an operative group mind is the shared belief that the four elements of earth, air, fire, and water have connections to the quarterly directions of north, east, south, and west. This is not a universal truth, but it is a functional truth for the members of an inner tradition who hold to such an agreement of consciousness. A group mind ensures that all the parts are working together in harmony for the greater good and common understanding. It also serves as a cohesive agent that maintains the inner mechanisms of the tradition. When inner mechanisms are repeated over a period of time, a powerful momentum of energy is created. During the course of this book the theme of "ancestral memory" and "morphic fields" will address this basic principle.

An inner tradition is, in part, a spiritual map. Simple examples of spiritual maps (as agreements of consciousness) are such things as horoscope charts, Tarot cards, oracle systems, ritual magic techniques, and so on. The people who practice these things understand them together in a commonality of conscious agreement. But these systems also possess greater depth, and within these systems are found advanced levels of inner traditions.

Once an inner tradition has been successfully formed and operated, it is aligned at this stage with *inner planes* realities. What this means is that it operates and functions in both this world and the other world. For the members of the tradition it exists and functions as a meeting place between the worlds; its structure allows them to interface with other dimensions and the beings that occupy them. This is not as difficult as it may sound, and the purpose of this book is to guide you to fully accessing the inner traditions presented through its pages.

For centuries, inner traditions have been hidden from the public, or if not hidden have been presented in ways that made them appear to be something else. This is perhaps no more apparent than in fairy tales and in the old myths and legends of our ancestors, particularly those associated with magical and mystical themes. The old stories appear at the same time to convey different meanings reflected in an outer form and an inner form of the tales. The outer form is the story itself, which seems to entertain and even to convey a message or social moral. The inner form transmits a code or a set of keys designed to access a much deeper level. This is because enlightenment does not dwell on the surface; it dwells in the depths below. It is what brews inside the mystical cauldron.

A very ancient concept known to our ancestors was the idea that light is at home in the darkness. From this notion arose myths about deities of the sun and moon coming up from the Underworld and then returning there again after journeying above the world of mortal kind. These great spheres of light were at home in the Underworld, and the oldest tales of the Underworld speak of it possessing stars, a sun, and a moon. This is also mentioned in old tales about the hidden Faery Realm, which was often secreted inside mounds or mountains.

Many modern people imagine the Underworld to be a dark and foreboding realm. Indeed, some old stories do seem to portray it in this manner. But within the inner tradition the Underworld is the starting point for those who seek enlightenment. Very deep levels exist here, and it is from the darkness that we discover light. This is apparent in the ancient tales that require heroes to journey to the Hidden Realm in a sacred quest.

Many years ago, while I was researching cauldron myths and legends from various European regions, I discovered a striking commonality at their core. Magical and mystical cauldrons are always hidden away within a cave, a dungeon, or the Underworld. A journey is required to retrieve them, or a task is necessary to prove the seeker worthy of winning the cauldron. But central to all the stories is the idea that the cauldron is lost or stolen, and is in need of retrieval or rescue. In the Christian era, the ancient cauldron mysteries were adopted by the mystical tradition of Christianity where they become the mysteries of the Holy Grail. The Grail mythos shares the same cauldron theme wherein the Grail must be retrieved through a holy quest.

While reading these old stories, I was left wondering why the tales were always about lost or hidden cauldrons. The general themes left the impression that a previous state of enlightenment or power was either lost or stolen, and was no longer to be found in its previous location in the mortal realm. This seemed odd to me, because we tend to think that our ancestors lived and breathed the ways that many Neo-Pagans now seek with all their hearts. So what was it that our ancestors felt was lost or stolen in their own time of magic and enlightenment? What were the storytellers trying to say?

What I came to believe is that these stories were not meant for the people of the time in which they were first spoken or written down (at least not in the way we might think). They were meant to be passed on to a future time where their meaning could bring the reality of what seemed to be a fabled enlightenment. In this regard, the bards were the stewards of esoteric tradition and the prophets for a coming new age. I believe they foresaw the time when the *One God* would come to displace the *Many*. This is almost certainly suggested in the Sibylline Books, which many people regard as prophesying the coming of Jesus and the rise of Christianity.

It is possible that the tale of the lost cauldron is in a large part a message about finding what you sense is lost or missing in the depths of your spirit. But it is also a tale of hope in which devoted effort assures results. Perhaps the ancients were saying that when you feel something is missing or stolen, go deep into that void and retrieve what is lost. Seek and find the lost cauldron of inspiration, enlightenment, and renewal.

The quest of the lost cauldron always requires a journey involving a descent into a dark place or realm. On a mundane level, when we are deeply sad, hurt, or depressed, we tend to go inward. From this inward descent we dwell for a while in isolation and in personal darkness. This is a stage of depression, and the word itself refers to sinking below, which is reflective of the downward journey to retrieve the lost cauldron. It is in this place, or mental state, that we become renewed and pass back into the world of light. However, in the inner tradition this is not about self-help, psychology, or therapy, it's about inner planes contacts that establish altered states of consciousness.

If we place the mythos of the lost cauldron into a category, then it must reside in the Underworld traditions of our ancestors. In contemporary thought, enlightenment is almost always associated with the heavens or Overworld. Enlightenment is often viewed as associated with the heights. However, in the earlier inner traditions enlightenment is the obtainment of the balance of light and darkness (a spiritual equinox, if you will). But we must be careful not to confuse darkness with negativity. Equally, we must also be careful not to equate "good" with "above" and "bad" with "below." Part of enlightenment is the knowledge that darkness is not the absence of light, and light is not the absence of darkness. We catch a glimpse of what seems to be a paradox when we consider that the color black is the presence of all colors, and white is the absence of all colors. Therefore things are not always what they appear to be on the surface.

The color white has long been associated with death, due to the natural coloration of bone. White appears in connection with cauldron tales in several ways. One example is the name Ceridwen, one of the classic cauldron keepers ("wen" means "white" in Celtic terms). Her cauldron was attended by nine virgins, wearing white dresses, and the rim of the cauldron was decorated with thirteen white pearls. In many cauldron tales, bones are placed in the cauldron and are returned to full living human form. This theme is featured in various tales such as that of the witch known as Medea.

Unlike the usual cauldron tale of inner tradition, the witches' cauldron is not typically lost, nor is it hidden in the Underworld. Medea's cauldron is placed in the world of the living, and she tends it at night in a remote place beneath the stars and moon. This theme can be regarded as one indicating that the cauldron mysteries survived the displacement of paganism under Christianity and were passed on in witchcraft traditions. Therefore the cauldron mysteries did not require retrieval by the members of the witches' sect. Instead, the inner mysteries of the witches' cauldron were obtained following formal initiation as opposed to a quest into the Underworld—although the two concepts cannot truly be separated or regarded as non-related.

The inner tradition of cauldron mysteries includes several very important vessels and the tales connected to them. Among the best known are:

- The Cauldron of Dagda, from which no one comes away unsatisfied.
- The Cauldron of Ceridwen, which brews a potion of enlightenment and great wisdom.
- The Cauldron of Ceres, which creates a brew of enlightenment and ushers in initiation into the inner mysteries.
- The Cauldron of Bran, which heals and restores life.
- The Cauldron of Medea, which renews life.

The themes of renewal and regeneration are central to the ancient tales connected to these magical or mystical vessels. This fact has continually brought my thoughts back to the message of the bards that I previously mentioned. Today we find a great deal of effort directed to the reconstruction of ancient pagan traditions, beliefs, and practices. This is, in many ways, an attempt to restore the hearts and minds of our ancestors who lived and breathed the things sought now by reconstructionists and others. However, the good news is that we don't have to reconstruct, we need only retrieve what has already been passed to us. To accomplish this we need to look inward to the very essence of our being.

You may not have ever thought much about the gift passed to you from your ancestors. Everyone is aware that we possess our physical traits because of the DNA passed to us though direct bloodlines. In other words the color of our skin, hair, and eyes comes from the physical traits of our ancestors. The same is true regarding our basic form, height, intelligence, and other things yet to be discovered by science.

I want you to stop now and think about something for a moment. You exist in material form because your direct ancestors survived long enough to reproduce. Therefore, within you is the DNA material that has passed through many generations. Try to imagine these generations as people lined up in a row, leading from you far back into the past. Literally thousands of people passed your bloodline on to you. Through this bloodline you share the culmination of the lives of your ancestors. You are their living representative and the bearer of the life blood of all who have gone before you.

There is something else I want you to consider at this point, in relationship to your DNA. We know that DNA is the hereditary material that carries and passes on the genetic information that ultimately determines the physical makeup of our bodies. This creative information is stored as a DNA code made up of four chemical bases. It is interesting to note that in metaphysics there are four creative elements responsible for manifestation: earth, air, fire, and water.

Our DNA was passed on to us directly from the material bodies of our ancestors. Energy exists within this DNA, whether in the form of electrons, chemical reactions, or whatever else may be at work. Some portion of the life energy of our ancestors is also passed to us within that DNA. This energy is part of the recording, transferring, and replicating process of DNA. What I want you to consider is that you pos-

sess the *energy imprint* of ancestral memory down to the cellular level of
your entire being. Metaphorically speaking, this is the sacred cauldron
hidden in the deep recesses.

As we know, our DNA is bound into a form called a double helix,
which has the appearance of a long spiral staircase or a twisted ladder. Spirals have long been associated with transformation, and in the
Underworld tradition the spiral stairway is featured in many stories
related to accessing the Underworld and finding the lost cauldron. It
is certain that the ancient people who passed on such tales did not have
our modern knowledge of genetics. However, the spiral itself appears to
be a sign of inner awareness on some level. It is a representation of the
sacred force that permeates existence.

The image of the double helix is similar in form to the caduceus of the
god Hermes or Mercury, who was a messenger of the gods. The classic
caduceus has two snakes winding around a center rod or wand, which

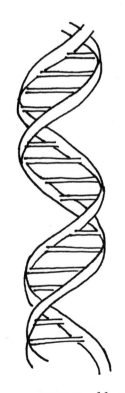

Figure 1: DNA Double Helix

has come to mean good health. In addition to being a messenger, Hermes was also the guide of departed souls entering the Afterlife. In this light the intertwined spiraling snakes on his wand symbolize the intertwined mystery of life and death. The double serpents on the caduceus also resemble the double helix of the DNA spiral. In this one symbol we can see the DNA theme as it relates to genetic messages and to the connection between past and present generations—the gift of the dead to the living. But like the twin serpents that symbolize life and death, there are two things to consider here.

In some circles of Neo-Pagan thought it is believed that many serious health issues are rooted in the notion that our ancestors have handed down to their descendants the disharmonious energies of their negative life

Figure 2: The Caduceus of Hermes

experiences. The negative energy inherited from our ancestors is static and does not function for the wholeness of the intent of our DNA. Therefore some people believe this to be the reason we are seeing so much disease and imbalance in the human vessels of the current age. However, this belief also focuses on how we handle negativity in our own present lives.

The tenet holds that when we have negative or positive thoughts that affect us emotionally we produce a vibration that can be felt or sensed by the people around us. It even passes into the objects within our home or workplace; but more importantly this energy also affects the cells and DNA within our being. The risk is that this negativity will awaken the ancestral memory of disease that was passed through the genetic memory of our DNA. If so, then our cells replicate this memory from the stored DNA message, and we find ourselves suffering from a hereditary condition like cancer or some other disease. This demonstrates that it is important for us to strive to elevate our spiritual condition and nurture our most selfless traits.

A vital element in lost cauldron tales is the ethical and moral character who takes on the quest. The spirituality of the seeker is important because he or she must, on some level, possess the essence of what awaits within the cauldron's brew. Celtic legend mentions certain cauldrons that will not boil food for a coward. This tells us that the heart and mind of the cauldron seeker must possess desirable traits. In this light we can see the idea reflected that our DNA responds to the condition of our mind, body, and spirit. We must not awaken the negative things passed to us from our ancestors, but we must (through what is noble within us) draw up the richness of the true elixir simmering in the hidden cauldron.

It is well known that the power of the mind and the intense will of an individual can contribute to health or illness. In this light the metaphor of the need to retrieve the lost cauldron of renewal and regeneration becomes very clear. For us, the quest for the cauldron is an inward journey to retrieve ancestral knowledge and wisdom. In the following chapters you will discover a number of exercises and guided imagery sessions designed to help you achieve this goal.

In metaphysics there is a principle known as "like attracts like." This means that a magnetic energy arises when one thing comes into proximity with another thing that shares the same nature. The principle applies equally to things that are positive or negative. If we lend a continuous stream of energy to the belief or fear that a specific thing will go wrong, then we encourage its manifestation. Likewise, if we focus our energy on things we desire, then we attract them into our lives. It is as if the Universe is listening, and in this case our feelings are the unedited messages of what we desire. The Universe responds by sending things to us that match those messages. It doesn't distinguish between good and bad, because it has no judgment. When we raise negative energy, the message is that we want negative things to manifest in our lives. When we raise positive energy, then the message is that we desire positive things to manifest.

Applying the principle of attraction (like attracts like), I have incorporated into this book a variety of ancestral practices, tools, and concepts. By working with these things you can awaken the ancestral correspondences within you. With good effort you can create lasting alignments that will fortify your spiritual journey. This is a step-by-step process—I strongly encourage you not to skim through the book or pick and choose which exercises to perform. I must stress that this work is a process, and there is no single exercise in this book that is *the one* that will deliver what you seek.

If you regard the pages of this book as the footsteps on your journey to obtain the lost cauldron, then you will arrive fully prepared. Leaping ahead or flipping through the book is like taking a shortcut that ends up far from where you meant to go. It can even lead you into a thicket where you become stuck and can progress no further.

In ancient tales, there is a theme about being "fairy led" into a thicket and becoming lost. It is all too easy to drop our work and chase our delights. But when the hero is mindful of purpose and intent, and is not willing to give in to distraction and temptation, then he or she bypasses the pitfalls and arrives in good time at the desired goal.

With all this in mind, we'll move on to the next chapter and explore the concept of ancestral wisdom. Once this understanding has been established you will be ready to move on to the following chapters, which present the practical work, exercises, and applications. This present chapter and the next are designed to supply the foundation.

FOUR

ANCESTRAL MEMORY

The ancient myths and legends of our ancestors contained more than just quaint tales and moral lessons. They also recorded the beliefs, perspectives, hopes, dreams, and aspirations of the people who preserved and passed the old stories on to another generation. In this light they can be regarded to a certain degree as an ancestral memory scrapbook. In other words, these are the spiritual memories of the good old days as reflected through the spiritual journey taken by our ancestors.

In this chapter we will examine the idea of genetic memory in the context of what is passed from one generation to another. Having this understanding will help us see the reality of what the exercises in this book can accomplish. In essence, genetic memory and myth and legend are (metaphorically speaking) two strands of message carriers (like the double helix of the DNA spiral). All we need to do is break the code, at which point darkness turns to light and we arrive in front of the hidden or lost cauldron of our ancestors. We can then drink from the sacred brew contained within the cauldron or immerse ourselves in the bubbling liquid of renewal and regeneration.

One of the goals of this chapter is to demonstrate that the passing on of ancestral memory within our DNA is not a fanciful notion. Instead it is rooted in a deeper and expanded understanding of biology. Biology, as a science, can only measure and verify things that are within the scope of current technology. Science cannot measure or verify things such as the existence of a soul or that of a divine being. This does not mean that such things do not or cannot exist. It simply means that we do not possess the tools that are necessary to allow us to make an objective scientific ruling.

In the absence of science and physics, we can do more than wait around for technology to catch up with the answers we seek. For centuries we have possessed a metaphysical science and an occult technology. This provides us with the subjective experience, which is the other half of understanding reality. Relying solely upon objectivity is like never considering that a tree has a root system because it cannot readily be seen. To gain a full comprehension of the tree we must take a leap of faith and dig deeper to see what, if anything, lies hidden from our view (our current knowledge and assessment). This is how hidden roots are discovered.

I want to turn now to a brief examination of two important concepts: genetic memory and morphogenetic fields. A full comprehension of these subjects is not possible in the scope of this present book. You can research these topics further on your own as you wish by using the Internet and the pertinent books listed in the bibliography provided in the back of this book. In the meantime I offer you my understanding and personal experience related to the subjects.

I want you to have an understanding of these concepts before you begin working with the exercises in this book. I liken this to writing a cookbook. If I only give you recipes and offer you nothing about how spices and flavorings enhance specific things, then I limit you to the meals detailed in the book. But if I show you the "how and why" of cooking with this and that, and provide you with an understanding of nutrition, then you can go on to create your own tasty and nourishing meals. With this in mind, let's move on to understanding a couple of important components that support the work ahead.

DNA and the Ancient Serpent

It is well known that the DNA spiral resembles the basic form of a serpent. In many shamanic traditions the serpent plays a significant role related to inner journeys of exploration and enlightenment. The serpent is frequently a creator being and is associated with the sky and the earth. Several anthropologists, including Jeremy Narby and Michael Harner, have written about their serpent experiences while living among primitive tribes in South America. Under the influence of hallucinogenic potions, the anthropologists saw visions of giant serpents that spoke to them about the origins of the world and the life upon it. Despite living among different regional tribes, the hallucinations were strikingly identical, both in terms of the appearance of the serpents and the imparted teachings.

The shamans who worked with the anthropologists spoke of various things that helped them access the worlds above and below, variously described as a vine, a rope, or a ladder. Among European shamans, we also find the reported use of a spiral staircase to access the worlds. These tools not only allow access to the other worlds, they also make it possible to communicate with spirits. It is noteworthy that these methods of accessing information all have the appearance of a DNA spiral.

Our DNA contains a mystery. Science only understands about one third of the DNA spiral, which is the portion that contains the instructions for creating a human being. The rest of the DNA spiral is referred to by the majority of scientists as "junk DNA" (a dismissive perspective that actually means they do not know or understand the purpose of the majority of the DNA strand). However, scientist Carl Sagan, in his book *Shadows of Forgotten Ancestors* (1992), suggests that the unknown portions of our DNA may be the remains of genetic instructions that were important for our distant ancestors, but now appear to be obsolete. It is likely that in the future, scientists will discover what is hidden and vital in the remainder of the DNA spiral.

Narby notes that, like the serpents of hallucinatory experience, DNA lives in water and is a being of transformation. The serpents seen by the anthropologists were described as shining and brightly colored. Narby writes about the fact that DNA emits photons that create a coherent source of light in the same way as a laser beam does. This makes it possible for the photons to form three-dimensional holograms. Narby suggests that this inner source of light may be the agent that forms the appearance of the serpents, and gives them their brilliance as well as three-dimensional form. If so, then the shamanic encounter with the serpents is an inner journey into the energy of the DNA. This is, in fact, what Narby points to, saying that shamans take their conscious-ness down into the molecular level. It is there that they gain access to information communicated from DNA. This, Narby proposes, is what the shamans describe as talking to the spirits.

In many of the old inner traditions, spirits are the ancestors of past generations. It was an ancient practice to call upon these spirits for ora-cle knowledge. One of the most famous of the ancient oracle traditions was that of Delphi, where oracle abilities were made possible by breath-ing the intoxicating fumes. One legend describes these fumes as rising from the decaying body of a giant python that lay deep in a dark pit. This theme, of course, is a metaphor of the Underworld realm of the dead.

The belief in oracles was rooted in the idea that the dead were fur-ther up the road than were the living, and could therefore see the future. They could look back to the mortal realm and pass on the knowledge of forthcoming events. But do the dead exist in another realm from which they can send messages to us? Or do they reside within our DNA? Per-haps the answer to both questions is yes, and that DNA is the portal guarded by the mystical serpent.

Genetic Memory

In the context of this book, genetic memory is the theory that within our DNA resides memory imprints from our ancestors. The idea behind this genetic memory is that an individual's experiences are imprinted upon his or her cells and are carried in the DNA where they lay hid-den within the material passed on by their descendants. This idea can be extended into understanding how it is that birds know how to build nests, how spiders know how to weave webs, and so on. This area of study is what those who study animal behavior call the *innate releas-ing mechanism* (IRM). Joseph Campbell, in his book *Primitive Mythology* (1991), describes this principle in telling the story of sea turtles.

Campbell describes how hundreds of sea turtles are born at a particular time in the sands just above the tide line. On the precise day of their birth, a huge flock of sea gulls circles overhead. The gulls quickly descend and pick off the tiny turtles as they race to the relative safety of the water. What is interesting here is that the newborn turtles appear to already know several things at birth. They know in which direction the water lies and that they have to get to it quickly. But more importantly they already know how to swim when they first enter the water. They have no previous knowledge of any of these things because they have never experienced them before. Yet they are clearly directed by something within to get into the water as rapidly as possible and swim away. Most scientists believe this is nothing more than a mindless series of reactions to internal chemicals being released due to external stimulation. If so, it is a remarkable coincidence that this mindless interplay just happens to ensure the survival of the species.

In a related study of animal behavior mentioned by Campbell is the account of newly born chicks. Studies show that the chicks will dart for cover when the shadow of a hawk passes near them, but they do not have the same reaction to the shadow of a duck, pigeon, or some other bird that doesn't prey on them. Campbell calls this the "inherited image of the enemy," and says that this threatening image lies sleeping in the nervous system, awaiting the proper stimulus to evoke it. This demonstrates the theme of ancestral memory hidden within the DNA.

Reportedly, human beings also possess "innate releasing mechanisms," as do other animals as well. But, as Campbell notes, instinctive behavior in humans is more open to learning and conditioning than it appears to be among other animals. In humans, individual experience can alter or control instinctive reactions to a much larger degree than is demonstrated by other terrestrial life forms.

A new field of study known as morphogenetics strongly suggests that what we think of as instinct is really an inherited memory that resides in our DNA. In this light, a spider knows how to build a web, and a bird knows how to construct a nest because they receive this information from the memories of their ancestors. This is transmitted through an energy called morphic resonance.

Morphic Resonance

For many years I have taught a principle that I call "the momentum of the past." The idea is that when an action is performed in the way it has been done repeatedly over the centuries, it builds up a momentum of energy like a cresting ocean wave. Therefore by performing the ancient practice we attract this energy or we align to it. It then pours from the past into the present and washes over us.

In the field of morphogenetics we find an almost identical principle known as morphic resonance. The theory is that a field is created by repeated actions or habits. This energy field carries the memory and the instructions of these things. In other words, the patterns are absorbed and retained in a cohesive field of energy. Living beings draw this energy to them like radio waves to a receiver. This energy then influences the beings through the transmission of informative instructions contained within the field.

One example of responding to morphic resonance is the migration of animals. Response to morphic resonance includes other things that scientists call instinct. Scientists do not believe that nature contains any intelligence of its own, nor does nature have a goal or an intended purpose. As previously noted, scientists see nature and its inner mechanisms as things that operate mindlessly through a series of chemical reactions to a variety of stimulus. Pagans regard nature and its processes in a completely opposite way. They perceive divine consciousness within all things, which gives meaning and direction to existence. Scientists view existence as a perpetual motion machine that somehow created itself and has no conscious goal or intention.

Morphic Fields

In The Witches' Craft (2002), I wrote briefly on the idea of morphogenetic fields. The theory of a morphogenetic field was first proposed in the 1920s and was most recently expanded and popularized by the British biologist, Rupert Sheldrake.

The theory is that every organism is surrounded by an interconnected energy field, which transmits information in one form or another. Sheldrake suggests that the evolution of a species begins when members in one location are subjected to environmental changes. Information regarding these changes is transmitted on to stable environments not yet influenced by the catalyst. As a result, the information transmits ahead the need to adapt, and the process of adaptation begins in response. It is known, for example, that trees surrounding a diseased tree will thicken their leaves and bark to protect against the spread of infestation.

The concept of the morphogenetic field is similar to the basic theory known as the *hundredth monkey*. This controversial idea proposes that once a large number of individuals engage and maintain a certain practice found to be functional and effective, they reach "critical mass" and a new cultural awareness arises. This new awareness is somehow communicated directly from mind to mind over great distances without any apparent connection, bridge, or known means of conveyance. This results in the same practice arising within cultures that have no direct contact with each other. Some people find evidence of Jung's concept of the Collective Unconscious in such phenomena, and have used this observation as evidence that an ideological breakthrough occurs when enough individuals in a population adopt a new idea or behavior.

One of Sheldrake's theories suggests that societies have social and cultural morphogenetic fields that organize behavior. In essence these fields influence individuals to act as one unit in a commonality of action and expression. One example is a flock of birds in flight. The birds move together, with each individual turning in unison with the flock as though it is one single organism.

Sheldrake states that tests have been conducted on the reaction time of individual birds using a stimulus to assess the speed of a single bird's response time. The tests determined that the maximum reaction time of an individual bird is less than the time required to turn in harmony with the flock. In other words, an individual bird could not turn on its own in flight (in reaction to a stimulation) as quickly as the flock turns as a synchronized whole. Something else is at work in the mechanism of birds moving in shifting flight formations. A message is being received by each bird simultaneously, and therefore the birds are not reacting to the movement of the bird next to them. Each bird is instead directed to move precisely at the same time and in the same direction as all the rest of the birds. They move under the influence of a morphogenetic field.

An important element of morphogenetic fields is that they form around groups of people who think and behave in unified ways. Sheldrake refers to this as the creation of a social organism, and he suggests that this is reflective of the hive mentality of wasps and bees. In this sense, morphogenetic fields unite individuals and they influence or facilitate how they work together. When this becomes functional the members develop into a social organism, a family unit with a common goal or function.

The idea of communication and morphogenetic fields also ties in with interesting recent discoveries related to DNA. Scientist and New Age writer Gregg Braden presented an experiment program on his personal website. These experiments were reportedly conducted by the military in a program developed by a scientist named Cleve Baxter (details appear in The Journal of Mind-Body Health, volume 9, 1993).

In the experiment, white blood cells were collected from DNA donors and placed in chambers where they could be monitored through electrical changes. In the experiment the donor was placed in one room and subjected to emotional stimulation that consisted of a selection of video clips presented to generate a variety of emotions in the viewer.

As part of the experiment the donor's blood cells were placed in a different room within the same building occupied by the person. Both the donor and his cells were monitored at the same time during the experiment. The results demonstrated that as the donor exhibited emotional peaks or valleys as measured by electrical responses, his blood cells in a separate room exhibited the identical responses at the exact moment. There was no lag time between responses and no transmission time took place. The reaction of donor and blood cell sample was simultaneous.

According to Braden, the military then wanted to see how the factor of distance between donor and DNA might affect the results. The experimenters reportedly ceased testing after even fifty miles of separation made no difference in the results of the experiment. Distance seemed to have no effect on the reaction of donor and DNA. The conclusion was that living cells communicate through a previously unrecognized form of energy that is not affected by time and distance.

The theme of the experiment described by Braden is not an isolated one. Sheldrake's theory of morphogenetic fields includes the idea that interconnectedness exists even at great distances. One premise is that even when a member of a group that shares a morphogenetic field (in the sense of a social organism) travels away, he or she still remains part of the group. In other words, no matter how far away the individual is, he or she is still subject to the influence of the morphogenetic field that's attached to the group of individuals as a whole.

When we consider this principle, it seems to apply to the magical notion that a person can be affected through a spell that employs a poppet containing fingernail clippings or hair from the target person. In this case it is the DNA that unites the specimen with the donor, and it is the morphogenetic field that transmits the influence.

It is this personal connection that is at the heart of the idea of ancestral memory. We do not internally possess the memories of everyone who ever lived on the earth (although we can access the *collective* through morphic resonance). We directly possess only the memories of our blood relatives. However, this does not negate the idea that we also possess what are called "soul memories," accumulated over many lifetimes spent in a variety of different blood lines. It is interesting to note that a belief exists in many old witch families that a soul can chose to return within the same blood line and live again as a descendant. This is, in part, the importance of witch blood in some family traditions.

Past Life Recall

The idea of recalling a past life is, of course, related to the belief in reincarnation. The belief that a person has lived before provides comfort that he or she does not perish at death. It also offers liberation from the idea that a soul can be imprisoned and punished for eternity in some hellish realm of existence.

It is a common experience for very young children to make references to a previous life. Some will talk about brothers or sisters that do not exist at present. Others will say things to adults like "*When I was the mommy and you were little,*" and then go on to describe some situation. Most people dismiss this behavior as imaginary or playful. Others regard it as evidence of past life recall.

One question that arises when we consider the concept of reincarnation is whether we are meant to remember past lives or not. If we are meant to recall past lives, then why is this information not readily available to us; why do we not easily remember? Does the memory of the past leave us because it is dismissed by the adults we rely on in our childhood? In other words, does the suppressive influence of adults that discourage talk of past lives cause children to forget or stifle the memory of past lives? Or is it a natural occurrence within the cycle of life?

For the purposes of this book we will focus on genetic memory as opposed to soul memory (although the latter will be discussed in other parts of the book as well). It should be noted that genetic memory and soul memory can go hand-in-hand regarding souls that return to specific blood lines. One theory is that souls travel in groups, reincarnating in ways that ensure they will meet one another again. However, the relationship roles they formerly experienced are shifted, and gender often rotates with each incarnation. The latter is an indication that souls are not naturally female or male beings.

When we think of past life memories, we tend to think of them as cohesive and stored away. The idea is to awaken them in the belief they will then become part of our total recall. We can liken this to some stimulus causing us to remember something that happened to us when we were four years old. Genetic memory, in the form of ancestral memory, does not seem to operate in this way. It seems instead to be a holistic and fully integrated memory of one entity containing many beings, as opposed to a recollection of separate and individual beings that lived distinct mortal lives.

When considering genetic memory, it appears to exist as a collection of isolated components that are not directly linked together into distinct memory chains. It is like the difference between the letters of the alphabet and fully formed words. The letters exist separately, but when drawn upon can form words that in turn create messages. It is the proper integration that renders intentional meaning.

There is another more technical analogy to consider when we talk about genetic memory in the form of ancestral memory. If you know a fair amount about how computer programs function, then you understand how the data in specific files can be retrieved. When a data file is saved to the hard drive of a computer, a path to it is created in order for the computer to be able to locate and retrieve the data. There is a specific sequence that allows the computer to locate the file and deliver it to the viewing monitor.

The secret to effectively retrieving ancestral memory from the data base of our genetic makeup is to know the appropriate sequence to initiate. Otherwise we can randomly awaken memories and end up creating fictitious constructions due to a false arrangement. We can liken this to trying to fit dinosaur bones together without any understanding of how they must actually join together to establish the reality of the creature's true form.

The exercises and techniques presented throughout this book are designed as step-by-step methods to follow a spiritual map created by our ancestors. The reason we want to do this is to gain the alignments to ancestral knowledge and wisdom. Our ancestors were more in touch with nature than the majority of people are today. They lived in "common cause" with nature, and from this they gained a sense of being that few of us possess today. Our ancestors understood themselves to be part of nature. Contemporary humans involve themselves with mastery over nature. This changes the relationship in very key ways.

When we look at the stories of our ancestors, their lives seem filled with contact and communication related to gods, spirits, and animals. In later periods we discover enduring beliefs within common folklore and superstition. In this we find attitudes about faeries, demons, ghosts and magic. Well into the Renaissance period, the belief that humans interacted with nonhuman entities was a reality. As belief in such things diminished over the centuries, so too did communication. With the loss of communication came separation, which was followed by total and complete disconnection. As a modern people we have divorced ourselves from the world our ancestors knew, and therefore we can no longer hear the spirit voices.

Several years ago I was watching a weather broadcast, which the TV station titled "storm watch." The weather person was very serious as he announced "We're on storm watch" and then proceeded to show people piling up sandbags around their homes and businesses, hammering planks over windows, and in general trying to secure and protect everything against the approaching storm. I thought about what I was seeing and it seemed like the storm was being perceived as some sort of alien monster stomping its way toward the human villages.

I thought of what I had previously studied about ancient cultures related to storms. One thing that came to mind was the fact that offerings were given to protect against weather damage, as were prayers to the storm (or a god of storms). This was direct intentional communication. This was an understanding of natural relationships between humans and the power of nature. It demonstrated, at its core, respect and reverence—not of a mindless weather pattern, but of something sentient. We have lost this connection in modern times, and as a result we are subject to nature as opposed to living together in a common cause. We need to retrieve the lost cauldron.

In order to restore communication, we must tap into the ancestral memories. The map we will use on our journey to retrieve the lost cauldron is a series of connections to spiritual stages of development that shaped ancestral knowledge and wisdom. The chapters ahead will provide the techniques to establish these connections.

We will move along the well worn path of ancestors, walking where they walked before us. This will lead us to the less traveled road, at which point we will clear a way through the hidden path. At our journey's end we will encounter the sacred and hidden cauldron, which is simmered over the glowing embers of ancestral memory.

In the chapter ahead you will work with the ancestral stone, an important key and connection to the sacredness of the land that gives us life, and to what dwells beneath and above it. The stone will help connect you with the beginning, the first awareness among our ancestors that we are one with nature. You will learn that the stone is the meeting place between the worlds, a shamanic doorway to what exists above and below the world of mortal kind.

The concepts of "above and below" are important aspects that aid access to other realms of existence. As an alignment exercise, imagine the sky above you. Visualize the blue sky and the sun. Next, picture the night sky with stars and then with the full moon. These are primal memories, for this was the very same sky that each of your ancestors looked upon when they lived in their own time. This concept of "above" is a perception of the limitless expansion.

Since ancient times, the concept of "below" has been associated with a subterranean realm populated by a variety of beings from myth and legend. It has also been associated with the dead, who are known as the Beloved Ones. Your pagan ancestors knew the realm of the dead as the Underworld. The concept of "below" is a perception of finite extension.

In addition to above and below, we also use the perceptions called north, east, south, and west. Various forces and spirits are associated with these directions. In later chapters we will explore this further. For now it is important that we understand the idea of "four directions" as a perception of the concept of "all around."

Mystical tradition ties all of this together with the idea of the sacred stone, which anchors all of these concepts and brings them together. This is related to the practice of erecting standing stones and creating stone circles. Moving on to the next chapter, we will explore the sacred stone.

FIVE

THE STONE OF REMEMBRANCE

In ancient times there existed what is called the *omphalos* stone (pronounced ohm'fal-lohs). This is a Greek word that means navel, as in the attachment point of the umbilical cord. It was an ancient belief that the omphalos stone came from the center of the earth (a place envisioned as primal fire). One of the most famous of these stones was housed at the ancient oracle of Delphi. The great omphalos stone at this site was marked with a coiled serpent. This symbolism reminds us of the DNA spiral and its serpent-like appearance. The connections do not stop here.

The fire goddess Hestia was associated with Delphi and in her iconography she is sometimes seated on the omphalos. In the most common depiction of Hestia, she is seated on a domestic hearth (and we'll explore her further in other chapters). A very common old practice was to place the umbilical cords of infants under the hearth stone. This touches upon the theme of the navel in connection with a sacred stone.

Philolaos, a fifth-century Pythagorean, mentioned that the omphalos denotes the umbilical cord, which joins the child to the mother just as a stem connects a plant to the nourishing earth. He also pointed out that each generation of men is rooted in the previous one, and that descendants are rooted in the soil of the family home. We know that Neolithic burial sites indicate humans carried stones with them from their homelands as they migrated to other areas. This strongly suggests the idea of the importance of origins, a generative center (which again ties in with the theme of DNA).

The ancient Greek writer Nonnos mentioned that the omphalos is the mid-navel axis, and that when the goddess Harmonia wove the veil of the universe, she placed a representation of the omphalos as the center piece and worked outward. The mystics of the Pythagorean sect used the omphalos to represent the seed or "first cause" of the universe. The iconography of the omphalos includes an image of an egg with a serpent coiled around it. The idea of a "first cause" connects with DNA in the sense of creation or duplication. DNA is, in essence, the "first cause" related to our material existence, and it is the center of our inner world.

In a myth linked to the omphalos at Delphi, we find that Zeus sent two eagles from opposite ends of the worlds. The point at which they met in flight was Delphi, and this place became the center of the world and was marked by the placement of the omphalos stone. Ancient carvings and paintings show the omphalos at Delphi flanked by two eagles. This myth reminds me of the fact that we receive our DNA from both parents who "meet together" and create a child (that becomes the center of their universe).

In one ancient tale, the Greek hero Orestes was purified by Apollo beside the omphalos, which symbolized for him a new birth and a reintegrated consciousness. A fourth-century vase discovered in southern Italy shows the omphalos decorated with the designs worn on the clothing of soothsayers. The idea of the ability to foretell the future is a theme well suited to DNA.

As the "center of the world," the omphalos stone was the connecting link between the worlds. It was also considered to make communication possible between the world of the living and the dead, and the gods of the Underworld. The ancient writer Varro mentions in various writings that the omphalos at Delphi was the tomb of the sacred serpent of Delphi, the Python. It is in this Underworld connection that the omphalos and the serpent take on more significance as something connected to the consciousness of our ancestors.

Since ancient times, rock and stone have been assigned great meaning, symbolism, and significance by our ancestors. In part this is related
to the endurance of stone as a marker, structure, or protective barrier. But
there is also another relationship of a mystical nature. This is reflected in
folklore tales about spirits that are bound or connected to stone in some
meaningful way. One example appears in Italian folklore, where a fairy
or goblin can be magically bound to a stone with a natural hole worn
through it. The stone is then carried on the person, who can call upon
the spirit helper at any time. Other tales tell of ghosts bound to the headstones of their graves, or bound to sacred sites and ancient ruins.

Sacred sites almost always feature stones to indicate them. The
presence of stones seems to bestow sanctity to the place in which they
reside. But they also seem to possess a *feeling* that is almost tangible.
Being in the presence of ancient standing stones is not unlike walking
amidst the headstones in very old cemeteries. It is an ancient belief that
the stones of the burial place of a powerful man receive power from
him. The same can be said for the great standing stones that have stood
witness to countless rituals and celebrations (and some of these sites
also contain burial grounds).

Sometimes a person who was powerful in life is buried near sacred
stones, thus connecting his or her spirit and the stone. In other cases,
the stone is believed to be home to a spirit that was never a living person, and it thereby acquires a mysterious quality directly from the spirit
entity. By analogy, the spirit in the stone is like the soul in a human
body. Occult traditions arose wherein a person who comes to *know* the
stone can gain access to the spirit. But stones also allowed access to
spirit realms outside of the material world. The omphalos was, by legend, one such stone.

According to legend the omphalos could take on various forms such
as a pillar, a cone, or an egg-like oval shape. It is the pillar that best suits
the interests of this present chapter. As a pillar at the center of the world,
the omphalos joins together all the three known worlds of ancient times:
the Overworld, Middleworld, and Underworld (also known as the Otherworld). In occult tradition, this pillar is a ladder uniting heaven and earth

with the Underworld below. Sacred objects are often called ladders when sanctified by some perceived action or visitation of a divine being. The omphalos is sanctified by its connection to Zeus, Gaea (the earth), and the giant serpent Python (the Underworld connection), for it was Zeus himself who established the omphalos as the center of the world. The ladder brings us full circle back to DNA in terms of the appearance of the double helix.

In this chapter we will be working with the ancient core concept of a sacred stone. An exercise is provided to align you with the stone, and other exercises will allow you to work with the stone in ways that will manifest altered states of consciousness.

Quite some time ago I stumbled upon a passage in the book known as the *Theogony*, which was written by a Greek bard known as Hesiod, sometime around 700 BCE. He very briefly mentions a rural pagan belief system that he refers to as the "teachings of oak and boulder." He dismisses them in comparison to teachings given to him by the Muses, who Hesiod claims were sent to him by Zeus, with instructions to record in writing the origins of the gods.

The lofty philosophical writings of Hesiod, and other Greek writings, are important works, but I was much more drawn to the primal idea of the teachings of oak and boulder. This ties in nicely with the fact that our primitive ancestors carried stones with them that were taken from the land of their birth. These stones were also buried with members of the tribe. We cannot prove what these stones meant to our ancestors, nor can we study any documents or literature from this prehistoric period that might give us some solid clues (because such things never existed in this time period). However, we can look to writings from later periods that contain the theme of stones being important items for humans (outside of building materials and weapons). Ideas and concepts survive non-literate periods, as evidenced by bardic tales or oral tradition that were eventually written on scrolls and later published in books. This is what I call "folklore as history," but that is the subject of a future book.

One of the earliest uses of stone that clearly indicate a religious, spiritual, or magical regard for stone is the figure known as a *herms*. A herms is a carved pillar with the upper half (or third) shaped like a god or goddess. In ancient times these were placed at a crossroads. The name became linked with the god Hermes who was, among other things, a god of roads (and later the commerce that depended on road systems). An ancient practice required travelers to place a stone at the crossroads as an offering to the herms. These stones were collected by the road builders and used to extend and repair the roadways. When we also consider that Hermes was a god who escorted the dead, it is tempting to suggest that the traditional coin given to the Ferryman of the Dead for payment of passage into the Underworld may be a practice rooted in offering a stone at the crossroads.

For the purposes of the following exercise we are going to use an ancestral connection to the stone and to the crossroads as a portal to the Underworld or Otherworld. As you work with this exercise I want you to focus on the symbolism related to the concepts described in the chapters you have already read. If you have skimmed these chapters, please stop and go back and read them thoroughly. Skim-reading a book is like walking past a restaurant, taking a whiff of the food cooking, glancing through the window as you pass by, and then telling your friends all about the taste of the food, the service, and the menu. In this analogy you have not had any real experience through which to gain an accurate understanding, and your impressions most likely have no basis in the reality of what is offered.

EXERCISE ONE: *Awakening the Stone of Remembrance*

For this exercise you will need the following items:

- One stone (no smaller than a coin the size of a quarter and no larger than a chicken egg). I do not recommend using a polished semiprecious stone. Instead choose a stone in its natural form. Do not use petrified wood or a fossil. The stone can come from the land of your ancestors or it can be local to the area of your birth or to the place you call home. Please do not chip away or break off a piece of stone from a sacred temple, standing stone, or some old ruins at any ancient sacred site. I understand the desire to possess something that special, but it is an act that desecrates the site. This ultimately means that you will not end up with a sacred thing in your possession. You will own something quite the opposite.

- One piece of oak wood (substitute only if you must) about a foot long or so. This will be used as a place to set the stone. In effect this will be a mini altar for the stone.
- A pin or needle (to prick your finger with)
- Some perfume or cologne that you use as a personal fragrance
- A metal lid from a jar (about the size of the palm of your hand)
- Matches
- A garden spade or small shovel (you will dig a hole in the soil at least six inches deep)
- A bowl of water (for rinsing and cleaning)
- A cloth for drying
- A metal coin (this will be left behind in the soil as an offering)
- A pouch for carrying and storing the stone

The exercise is performed at noon and then repeated on the night of the full moon. This can be done on the same day, or on two separate days. The entire work is best performed at a crossroads, and ideally the setting should be rural. However this can be done in a city park if the requirements of this exercise do not violate the local laws pertaining to park usage. For the purpose of this exercise, the crossroads is defined as a place where three paths meet, or where four paths intersect. In other words, this means where paths come together to form a Y or an X pattern.

To begin the exercise, dig a hole wide and deep enough to accommodate the stone. Leave the pile of earth aside for later use. Sit in front of the hole facing the direction of East, and then place the oak piece between you and the hole. Next, lay the stone on top of the oak. Sit comfortably and when you are ready, imagine a line of people representing your ancestors. This line extends from you off into the eastern horizon. Strengthen this by picturing some figures in specific costumes of period dress that would have been worn by your ancestors (all the way back to animal skins). If you have a mixed ancestry, incorporate the appropriate cultural imagery to include them all. Allow these images to form, seeing the last figure on the horizon wearing animal skins.

The next step is to place your hands, palms facing down, above the stone and oak. Slowly lower your hands toward these objects. As you do this, try to recall the feeling of pushing your hands into wet sand or mud. This will help you descend inward. Continue until your hands come into contact with the stone and oak. At this stage imagine that you penetrate the stone and enter directly into its center.

At the center of the stone is fire, the primal fire to which the origins of life and substance in the material dimension can be traced. This fire is the divine source of all things. It is the formless presence of divinity, free from the domestication that manifests when humans give outward appearance to their gods and goddesses. Therefore at the center of the stone is the spirit flame.

To connect with this concept, pour some of your perfume or cologne into the metal lid (two thirds full) and then light the liquid with a match. Hold the stone in your left hand, pressed between your index finger, middle finger, and thumb. Pass the stone through the flames of the fire three times (being careful not to get burned, and make sure to keep clothing away from the fire at all times). As you pass the stone through the flames, say these words:

I *evoke the ancient flame within the memory of the earth. Awaken now and join the worlds above, below, and in-between.*

Immediately place the stone down inside the hole you dug. Next, place the offering coin in the hole, and say:

Nothing may be received except that something is given. Nothing may be given without something received.

Pause for a few moments and then touch the stone with your left hand, saying the word "below." Next, remove the stone from the hole, and with your dominant hand lightly toss the stone up above your head as you say the word "*above*." Catch the stone when it falls back down, and say the word "*between*".

It is time now to take the pin or needle and prick one of your fingers.* Touch a drop of your blood to the stone and say:

As the lineage bearer of my bloodline, I invoke the memory or all who came before me. I join the memory of my ancestors to the memory of the fire within the earth.

Place the stone against your heart and say the words:

Though I am a child of the earth, my race is of the stars.

Move in front of the bowl of water, and looking at the water say these words:

Water, you are rain fallen from the heavens. You are wells deep within the earth. You are rivers and streams rushing over the land. Bring purity to the three worlds.

Wash your hands in the bowl of water. Next, wash the stone in the water and dry it off thoroughly. Then gently press the stone against the three power zones of your body:

- forehead (and say "*above*")
- genital area (and say "*below*")
- solar plexus (and say "*between*")

This completes the awakening of the stone and your alignment to its energy. Place the stone in a carrying pouch and keep it there when not in use. The next step is to connect your *Stone of Remembrance* to the ancient serpent.

---

* See the publisher's note on page vi regarding safe practices.

EXERCISE TWO: *The Serpent Alignment*

For this exercise you will need the following items:

- Your Stone of Remembrance
- A piece of white cord, nine inches long
- White paint
- A small artist's paintbrush

This technique incorporates the concept of the serpent as a messenger between the world of the living and the realm of the dead. It also draws upon the idea of the serpent as a revealer of hidden truths. In the inner mystery traditions there are three colored snakes, but for our purposes in this section of the book we will work with the white serpent.

The white serpent symbolizes the "wisdom of the bone" concept, which is rooted in the idea that the bone represents the wisdom of the life experience left behind after death. This is one of the reasons why skulls were venerated within the ancient mystery traditions. The skull represented the accumulation of life experience and was the repository of ancestral knowledge and wisdom.

To begin creating the serpent alignment, take the stone from its pouch and set in on a work area. Take the white cord and tie a knot in one end. Place it in front of the stone. Look at the cord and imagine it to be a white serpent (the knot represents the head of the serpent). Pick it up and coil it around the index finger of your left hand, and then say these words:

With this string around my finger twirled, I fashion a creature of the Otherworld (visualize the cord becoming a living serpent).

Unwind the string from your finger and wrap it around the stone, saying these words:

Serpent of the color white, bestow your secrets of the night. Bear to me within the stone, the memories from ancestral bone.

Press the stone between the palms of your hands (like hands in prayer) and leave a small opening between the thumbs. Speak the following words and then, with your breath, blow three times into this opening:

Breath of life, voice of the wind, enter out and enter in.

Unwind the string from the stone and then place both back on the workspace. Using the white paint, create the image of a serpent winding around the stone (or coiled in the center of the stone). Allow the paint to dry completely before using the stone in the ancestral alignment.

EXERCISE THREE: *The Ancestral Alignment*

For this exercise you will need the following items:

- An offering coin
- Your Stone of Remembrance
- The nine-inch white serpent cord
- A replica of a human skull (size unimportant)
- A red candle (sized to fit on top of the skull)
- A cultural link (anything associated with your lineage)
- Offering of food and drink (with a cloth covering it)

Place the skull on the center of your work area. Secure the candle to the top of the skull. Set your stone in front of the skull, and lay the white cord on top of the stone. On the work area place the cultural link to your ancestors along with the coin. The link can be anything that reflects your nationality, and you can place several items from different cultures. The item can be something as simple as a book, a flag, a figurine, an article of clothing, or a doll. The idea is to have something that you identify with as reflective of the nationality of your ancestors. To enhance the experience you can play some music that is associated with your ancestral lineage. Folk music is an ideal choice.

When you are ready, touch the cultural link and imagine a current of energy flowing from you into the object. After a few moments, say these words:

I reach back though my link to those who came before, to those whose blood I bear.

Light the candle on top of the skull, and imagine a current of energy flowing to you from the flame. After a few moments say these words:

I openly receive that which flows to me and within me, that which comes to me from those who carried the blood before me.

Remove the cloth from the offering of food and drink. Present it in honor of your ancestors. Sit quietly for a few moments during this phase. When you are ready to move on, place the coin in front of the skull (touching it). Then say these words:

Nothing may be received except that something is given, nothing may be given except that something is received. I offer this coin made of metal from beneath the earth, and I receive from you the secrets that are found in your hidden realm.

Extend both hands outward toward the skull (palms facing upward). Rest your arms on the work area and gaze into the candle flame. At this phase think about the candle flame as the representation of the life force of your ancestors. As you look at the skull you are looking back at your ancestors. More importantly you are meeting them in the present, and it is in the flame that life exists between the past and the present. Spend a few moments with this theme.

The final step for the ancestral alignment involves the white cord. Grasp the knotted end of the cord between the index finger and thumb of your right hand. Slowly drag it into the open palm of your left hand (this is called the receiving hand). As you draw the cord, say these words:

Sacred white serpent I call to you beyond the veil. Come and be a messenger between the worlds, between the living and those in spirit form (visualize the cord as a living serpent).

Now, coil the white cord in the palm of your left hand. Then take the stone and place it gently on top of the cord. Cup your hands as in the gesture of prayer, leaving a small opening between the thumbs. Say the following words and then press your mouth against the opening and slowly but deeply inhale:

Breath of life, voice of the wind, enter out and enter in.

Return the white cord and your stone to the carrying pouch. Thank your ancestral spirits for attending and ask them to return to their realm. Immediately blow out the red candle on top of the skull. Take the food and drink offerings outside and bury them or toss them on the earth (the latter is appropriate if animals are likely to feed on it). To complete everything, push the coin down into the soil. You can and should repeat the ancestral alignment once a year, on November Eve (no earlier than nine p.m., but no later than midnight). This will help keep the stone charged and aligned.

Working with the Stone of Remembrance

The idea of a sacred stone is not that we make it sacred, but that we create the realization that allows us to recognize its sacredness. Our distant ancestors experienced nature as sacred, and through this they possessed an understanding of the core sacredness of everything in their world. In time, the complexities of life within social structures diverted attention away from nature and into community. Here the common person became saturated with the daily demands and responsibilities associated with life in towns and cities. As a result, sacredness became something outside of daily life, and it was only the shaman, medicine person, or the wise men and women who kept the true understanding of sacredness. The average person therefore found sacredness within formal religion, often designating one day of the week to entering into an active relationship with sacredness (typically in the form of attending services at a church or temple).

Our ancestors used stone altars in ancient times and marked sacred sites with great standing stones. In the lore of the Hebrews, their god wrote laws or commandments upon stone tablets. In the book of Genesis (chapter 28, verse 22), we find mention of a stone pillar that was regarded as the house of God. In Genesis, the biblical character known as Jacob has a dream while sleeping on a stone for his pillow. Jacob dreams of a ladder that allows angels to ascend and descend between heaven and earth. The significance of such a ladder in mystical tradition is a theme we will explore further in other chapters. For now, it is the stone that holds importance for us.

What we find in the tradition of a sacred stone is the idea that it can contain the presence or consciousness of a deity or a spirit. This concept of the sacred stone is also connected to the notion that the person carrying the stone creates an intimate link with the stone and what it contains or represents. In some primitive societies, we find the belief that the spirit of the person carrying a sacred stone passes at death into the stone. The spirit then inhabits or is connected to the place where the stone is afterward placed. This primitive belief may be at the core of the practice of visiting the dead in a graveyard where their headstones are placed.

For the purposes of this chapter the idea we want to keep in mind while working with the stone is the concept of sacredness and of inner connection. In this way, the stone becomes a conscious and daily alignment with spiritual forces that exist outside of us as well as within us. One basic exercise to perform is to touch the stone to the forehead, lips, and heart area. This act symbolizes the connection to our thoughts, words, and feelings. We can ritualize this through a simple daily ceremony.

To begin, choose a specific time of day or night that works best for you. If possible have this be the time before you have to deal with getting ready for work or other duties. Remove the stone from its pouch and press it gently against your forehead, lips, and heart area, saying:

I bring my thoughts, words, and feelings under conscious control. I call upon my ancestors for wisdom, communication, and guidance.

Cup the stone in your hands in the prayer position, leaving an opening between the thumbs, and then say these words:

Breath of life, voice of the wind, enter out and enter in.

Press your mouth against the opening and inhale. This completes the daily alignment. Put the stone back in the pouch.

Another use of the stone is for "re-membering" things of the past that are lost or forgotten. This requires that you tie the white cord around the wrist of your right hand, and hold the stone in your left hand. If you are left-handed then you will want to reverse this order.

With the cord and stone in place you can perform research, draft ritual concepts and text, meditate, and perform other tasks of your choosing. The idea is that you are aligning yourself with ancestral currents of knowledge and wisdom, through which you can channel. This current is the practical use of the occult concepts known as the "momentum of the past" and "morphic field resonance," which are discussed in various chapters of this book.

Another use of the stone is for performing blessings. This is particularly useful for newborns in the sense of ancestral lineage. The blessing ceremony can be as simple as gently touching the sacred stone to the infant's forehead, lips, and heart area. You can add the following words as an affirmation:

May your thoughts be clear and creative. May your words be wise and eloquent. May your heart be strong and true.

In the remaining chapters of this book you will encounter other uses of the Stone of Remembrance. The most important use of the stone is in the Cauldron of Memory retrieval work described in chapter nine. To effectively work with the sacred stone, you will need to perform the series of exercises throughout the book. These will help align you with the forces that can empower you through the connections you will create as you progress. This will require personal effort on your part, as it should and must. The benefits will be returned in accordance with the dedication and passion you invest.

SIX

CORDS OF CONNECTION

The use of cords in magic and religion dates back to antiquity. Cords often appear in context with enchanted ropes and mystical ladders. In some magical traditions the cord is used to capture or fix something into place. It is from this idea that the term "spell bound" originates. One example is the binding or wrapping of a clay or wax likeness of an individual with a cord or string.

On a higher spiritual level, cords are used for shamanic journeys and for healing purposes. In the mystery tradition, cords are bridges, extensions, and representations of spirit projection (a means of sending the soul or inner spirit off on a particular quest). In this way, the cord is a means of communication and transmission.

The concept of a cord is both primal and intimate for humankind. As we grow in the fetus stage, we develop a spinal cord. This cord serves to join mind and body together through a complex system of internal communication. Another important cord is the umbilical cord, which allows the fetus to be nourished through the host body of the mother. In the mystical tradition there exists a belief that the soul is connected to the flesh body by a silver cord. This cord serves as a type of tether that allows the soul to journey from the body in astral projection or shamanic journey. According to occult teachings, the silver cord is automatically severed at death and the soul is thereby released from the flesh body it had inhabited in life.

In mystical tradition, cords are joined together to form a rope ladder. This type of ladder is used to access other realms of existence. In ancient Egyptian belief we find references to two mystical ladders; one ladder allowed descent into the land of darkness, and the other ladder permitted one to climb to the land of light. These were called the *ladder of Shu* and the *ladder of Horus*. Each ladder was composed of seven rungs and was associated with the moon. The combined rungs of the ladder equaled twenty-eight days, roughly a lunar month.

The ladder is often linked to a mound. In ancient Egyptian tradition we find mention of a ladder extending from the burial place to the boat of souls. This boat floated among the stars in the night sky (specifically in the Milky Way). Old Egyptian legends refer to the god Shu-Anhur who lifted up paradise and created a mound or staircase with steps to it in order that he might reach the heights. An image of this mound may be seen in Egyptian art depicting the figure of a pyramid with seven steps (called the ladder or staircase of Shu or Sut).

The god Shu-Anhur was, in his earliest form, a god of divine wind and was known as the uplifter. In art he often appears wearing a headdress comprised of four plumes, which sports a serpent piece to denote his celestial nature. Shu-Anhur is also shown carrying a cord. In Egyptian myth he is often referred to as the *breath of Ra*. It is here in the idea of Shu's ladder and his association with the breath that we discover an interesting connection.

In very old tales we encounter the ladder by which the wizard, witch, or conjurer reached the land of spirits. This ladder is described as something drawn out of or emitted from the mouth in the form of a thread. In essence we can think of this as the spirit in the form of a filament. This coincides with the concept of the Egyptian word *nef*, which refers to the soul as both breath and spirit. In this light, the substance drawn from the mouth of the shaman represents a kind of ladder that serves as the visible mode of ascent or descent for the soul.

The cord, in the form of a vine, appears among many primitive tribes and is often associated with a tree. The mystical tree or vine is sacred and forms a connecting link and medium of communication between the world of the living and the dead. In primitive belief it is generally used by spirits as a ladder to pass downward and upward from the land of spirits. In Ojibway legend, the sacred vine was attached on one end and entwined around a star. Many traditions contain accounts of attempts to climb such heavenly ladders.

The Sacred Tree

The concept of a sacred tree is common to most ancient societies throughout the world. Connected to the tree is a belief that it joins various worlds or is a bridge to other worlds. In folkloric tradition we find the inclusion of a portal in the trunk of the tree—a hollow opening, usually near the base of the trunk—that is often referred to as a Faery Door.

In the most primitive legends, the tree must be climbed in order to access other realms. In some traditions, hanging from the tree bestows enlightenment. This theme appears in the tale of Woden/Odin who hung upside down from a branch, and in the classic image of the Tarot card known as the *Hanged Man*. One of the most modern models is the death of Jesus on a cross (a tree) and his ascension into heaven.

The famous explorer Alfred Howitt, in an article on Australian ceremonies (from the *Journal of Anthropological Institute*, May, 1884) writes about the tree as a shamanic tool for reaching the heavens. According to Howitt:

> The Australian natives make use of the tree as a mode of ascent to heaven for the spirits of the departed. The wizards also profess that they go up to consult the spirits of the dead by ascending a tree. Some of them make a pathway for the spirits to ascend and descend the tree of earth and heaven by cutting out a strip of bark, taken spirally from the top of a large tree down to the ground.

In folkloric tradition, and in ancient myth and legend, we find two significant trees. One is the great World Tree (usually an ash tree) that comprises the universe (or in some way connects all things together). The other is a single sacred tree that marks a sacred site (or is under the protection of a specific deity). This tree is often an oak, walnut, or willow.

In mystical traditions, we find the symbolic tree in the form of the Silver Bough or the Golden Bough. These sacred and magical branches allow safe passage between the mortal realm and the "Otherworld" of myth and legend. The Silver Bough allowed safe passage into the Faery Realm, and the Golden Bough granted the same in the Land of the Dead. The primary difference between the two branches is that the Silver Bough is given as a gift (by the Faery Queen), while the Golden Bough needs to be obtained through a sacred quest. The latter is a test of personal character, while the former is a freely given gift of acknowledgment of the seeker's moral fiber.

At the core of the Sacred Bough mythos is the idea of one thing that connects the traveler to the mortal realm while he or she enters and encounters another dimension. It is the way in and the way back out. One shamanic tool that incorporates the tree symbolism with the mystical journey theme is a specific set of cords. These cords, when assembled, are known as the Sacred Tree (among other names).

Before instructing how to use the Sacred Tree cords, we must first understand the symbolism that is literally woven into it. The Tree cords are of three individual colors: black, red, and white. The black cord is limitless possibility. The red cord is vitality. The white cord is ancestral wisdom. The cords' lengths are the measurement from the inside of your elbow to the tip of your index finger. This represents extension, your ability to extend outward and inward. Before cutting the cords to length, add three inches to allow for shortening due to tying the knots.

In the next section you will make the Sacred Tree, joining the three cords together by tying three knots on one end. Each knot should be spaced about a finger's width apart. The three knots should take up less than half the length of the cords as shown in the illustration. If done properly you will have three short ends above the knots and three long strands beneath the knots. The upper threads are the branches of the Tree and represent the divine triformis principle, which includes the idea of the *Three Daughters of Necessity* (sometimes depicted as the Three Fates).

The lower strands of cord symbolize the roots of the Tree, which extend into the Underworld. The knots themselves signify the Three Great Worlds of ancient thought: Overworld, Middleworld, and Under-

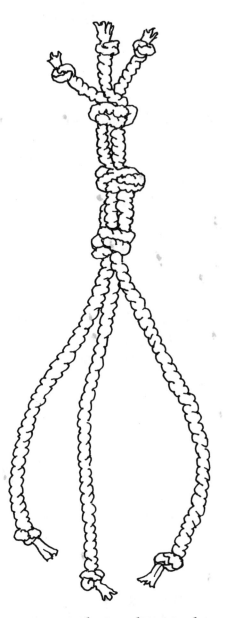

Figure 3A: The Sacred Tree Cord

world. The section where the knots appear represents the sacred ladder, and the trunk of the Tree itself. This instrument will become an important spiritual tool for your work in retrieving the "lost cauldron within" and the ancestral memory waiting inside.

Before moving on to work with the cords, it is important to say a few words about the Three Daughters of Necessity. Themis, the goddess of Necessity, brought forth three lovely daughters known as the Fates or the Moirai. In myth and legend all living things must eventually submit to these divine daughters. Their names are: Klotho, Lakhesis, and Atropos. Klotho spins the thread of life, Lakhesis determines its length, and Atropos cuts the thread when the time has come for death. The Three Daughters sit on three thrones and are dressed in white robes. The daughters wear garlands on their heads while they sing and turn a mystical implement. Lakhesis sings of past time, Klotho of the present, and Atropos of time that shall be.

In Plato's book (known as *The Republic*) we find in book ten the mention of "Necessity" in the sense of a being. In her lap is the *Spindle of Necessity,* which appears to be the inner mechanism of the Cosmos. Plato's description certainly more than suggests a connection to the known celestial bodies of the time: Stars, Sun, Moon, Saturn, Jupiter, Mars, Mercury, and Venus.

In working with the cords, we are dealing with the inner mechanism of the Cosmos. When the cords are made into the Sacred Tree we have, in effect, a spiritual ladder or bridge between the worlds. As a tool, our Sacred Tree is made up of the threads of Life, Death, and Rebirth. In braiding the three cords into one, we are also woven into the fabric of the Great Mysteries. Our lives then resonate with the harmony of the celestial bodies and the earth upon which we live. We join all of this to ourselves through the cords, with the realization that we are earth and stars, spirit and matter. We are finite and infinite at the same time. In this we discover that reality is simply the moment upon which our consciousness is focused.

EXERCISE FOUR: *Cord Alignment*

Required items:

- One black cord
- One red cord
- One white cord
- One red candle
- One white candle
- Your Stone of Remembrance
- Your favorite perfume or cologne

Set up your work area by placing the red and white candles near the back of the table or altar. Separate them by several inches and place the sacred stone between them. In front of this, lay out your cords, and then anoint the candles with your perfume or cologne. Then light the candles (be sure that the perfume or cologne is not near the top of the candle, nor on your fingers, when lighting the candles).

When you are ready to begin, construct the Sacred Tree from the three cords as previously instructed in this chapter. Lay the Tree on a work area, and take the long strand of black cord in your hand. Close your eyes for a few moments and imagine that you are surrounded by darkness. This is the beginning of all things, the dark womb from which all things are given birth. Next, imagine that a soft glow appears and you realize that you are in a huge cavern. This is the Underworld of myth and legend. Spend a few moments with this imagery.

Open your eyes, release the black cord, and pick up the red one. See yourself once again surrounded by the cavern. In the dim light you can see shadowy figures gathered all along a river bank. You notice that the waters of this river are red in color. Imagine that this is the river of ancestral blood, the vital force that flows from all of your ancestors throughout time. It also flows into the present and is in your veins. You now carry this into the future and will pass it on to another generation to come.

Hold the Tree in one hand, and with the other hand (using your index finger and middle finger) find the pulse in your wrist or neck. This is the sound of your ancestors walking and drumming; this is the echo of ancestral memory within you. Spend a few moments with this idea and focus on feeling a connection to those who came before you. They also felt the same pulse.

Set the Tree down, and then pick up the white cord. This cord represents bone, the ancestral remains within the physical dimension. When buried, the bones lie between the worlds of the living and the dead. In this context the white cord symbolizes the link between past and present.

While holding the cord in one hand, use the other to feel the bones in your body. Press your fingers along your skull and jaw bones. Then use them to feel your ribs. Next, feel your knee caps, shin bones, and then your feet. Spend a few moments realizing that the material composing your bones ultimately came from the material passed to you from your ancestors through a chain of DNA. In your skeletal frame you literally carry the link between you and your ancestors. Your bone marrow generates blood cells, which are created through the instruction of DNA. The "message" of your ancestors is alive in your blood. Spend a few moments thinking on all of this, and then place the Tree back on your work area.

Pick up your Stone of Remembrance, touch it to the three knots on the Tree, and say the following words prior to slowly blowing your breath across the stone and the three knots at each point:

Breath of life, voice of the wind, enter out and enter in.

Place the stone back between the candles. Pick up the Tree and hold it upright (short ends at top, long strands at bottom). Situate the Tree so that it dangles over the stone and between the candles (move them farther apart if they are too close to the cords and your hand). Focus your attention on the bottom cords and say:

Deep do the roots to the Underworld go, ancestral secrets rise upwards and flow (visualize a red river flowing upward into the dangling cords, which are bathed in the liquid).

Next, place the tips of your index fingers and thumbs of both hands on the cord area between the three knots. In other words your fingers are placed between the top and bottom knots (the center knot will therefore be between the fingertips of both hands). Bring your attention to this area by gently squeezing the cords, and then say:

In-between the worlds I stand, a walker of the sacred land (visualize yourself with the sun, moon, and stars above you, the earth beneath your feet, and the ocean below).

Now, hold the Tree up, suspending it from the three small cord tips at the top. Use your thumb and index finger to hold the cord in this fashion. With the same fingers of the other hand, squeeze each knot, beginning with the bottom one, and say:

Bottom knot: "*Below*" (visualize the Underworld as a cavern glowing with a soft peaceful light).

Top knot: "*Above*" (visualize the vast starry night sky).

Center knot: "*In-between*" (visualize the land, and in particular a site that you regard as sacred or holy).

At this stage it is time to extend the alignment to the concept of "all around." To do this, lift the Tree several inches above the candles, and move it slowly in a large circular motion around them, saying:

I touch the horizons, I touch the circle of the spheres, I touch the endless cycles (visualize the horizon in all directions as far as the eye can see).

Next lay the Tree in the palms of both hands, cupping it securely. When you are ready, present the entwined cords to each of the four directions, saying:

North: "*I call upon the elemental forces of earth to bestow foundation and stability*" (visualize things that you identify with these concepts such as mountains or boulders).

East: "*I call upon the elemental forces of air to carry messages to and fro*" (visualize the wind lifting a leaf upward or birds gliding on a current).

South: "*I call upon the elemental forces of fire to transform the mundane into the spiritual*" (visualize a gentle blue flame flowing over the cords like a calm, spreading liquid).

West: "*I call upon the elemental forces of water to give motion and direction*" (visualize a river flowing off into the distance).

To complete the alignment exercise, set the Tree cord down and perform the following. Place the Stone of Remembrance in the center of your work area. Lay the Tree around the stone in a circle. Lay your hands on top of these items and say:

> *I call to my ancestors. I join with the spirit of my ancestors. I walk with my ancestors. I walk for my ancestors. Together we are one.*

Return the stone to your pouch and put away all the items on your work area. Keep the Sacred Tree in a special place where it will not be touched by other people without your consent. From this point on you must treat the Sacred Tree with reverence. In other chapters you will be working with the cords in various ways.

Another important alignment involves the construction and use of a spirit cord. This alignment works with the theme of the shaman's ability to project his or her consciousness or spirit. As previously noted, we were formed in the womb with a spinal cord and nourished through an umbilical cord. An occult tenet states that we also possess a spiritual strand called the silver cord. For the purpose of this portion of the book we will consider the silver cord to be the "spirit cord" for the alignment work. Equating the two is not a formal tradition, but it does allow for another function of the cord concept.

The basic idea of the spirit cord is that it serves as a transmission for the consciousness. It is a physical mechanism that initiates a nonphysical process. In this sense it is just like any ritual or magical tool. Wielding it in the material world has its correspondence in the spirit world, astral dimension, or whatever one wishes to call it.

In shamanic tradition we find the ever-present concept of traveling between the worlds. As modern people we might rephrase this to say "shifting between states of consciousness." In any case, the journey is typically aided by a spirit guide. This being often takes the shape of an animal or some other creature. The serpent is among the most common forms used by spirits for this kind of task.

In Australia, some aboriginal shamans call upon a "rainbow serpent" which serves as a bridge between the earth and the sky. In some forms of Eastern mysticism, such as Tantra, a serpent of energy resides coiled at the base of the spine. Through prescribed techniques the serpent energy can be awakened, at which time it "climbs" up the spine into the center of consciousness in the brain. These two views seem to suggest there are different journeys, one an outer journey and the other an inner journey. If they are two different journeys, the suggestion is very strong that the mechanism and the intent are the same.

My own experience persuades me to believe that both journeys take place, and that the inner leads to the outer. What happens is that the "three-dimensional sacred geography" of the shamanic journey is made accessible through the concepts of "sacred physiology," in which case the material body that houses the soul becomes the doorway to three-dimensional consciousness. It is here we find that the way in is the way out, and vice versa.

The advantage of the spirit journey is that it allows us to enter directly into a pure realm uncontaminated with disbelief (whether our own or those of the people around us). In a world without disbelief anything is possible. Therefore, what we retrieve through a shamanic journey is the power to transform what is previously acknowledged as "reality" into something different, namely into limitless possibilities that appear contrary to the situation at hand. This is one way in which things such as "miraculous" healings take place.

EXERCISE FIVE: *Making Your Spirit Cord*

Required items:

- One nine-inch length of thin green cord
- Your white serpent cord
- Your Stone of Remembrance
- A bowl of spring water (about the size of a salad bowl)
- One live ivy plant
- A pinch of peppermint
- A pinch of lavender buds
- A pinch of mandrake root
- Two white candles
- One twenty-four-inch necklace (or length of cord to wear around your neck).
- A carrying pouch large enough to accommodate the cord and the herbs

Set up your work area with the white candles placed toward the back and separated apart. Between the candles set the sacred stone, and in front of this place the white cord. In the center of your work area set the bowl of fresh water. To the left of this, place the ivy plant. To the right of the bowl set the three pinches of herbs in a row: on the left is the peppermint, in the center is the lavender, and on the right is the mandrake. Set the green cord in the area closest to you.

Light the candles and then coil the white serpent cord. Set it upon the Stone of Remembrance. Put on the necklace, and then take the green cord and wrap it around the center of the necklace.

Immerse the fingers of both hands in the bowl of water. Slowly scoop up the water and allow it to trickle back into the bowl. Repeat this three times as you listen to the sound of the water. While performing this task, imagine yourself to be walking in a large cavern, and what you hear is the sound of water dripping down from the ceiling into small pools.

Using your wet hands, gently pat your forehead. Do the same for your solar plexus and then your genital area. Once you have finished, pick up the white cord and stone. Place the coiled white cord in your right hand and the stone in your left.

Visualize the white cord becoming a living serpent, several feet long. It moves from your hand, coils its tail around your wrist and then gently, but forcefully, pulls and leads you off to a journey. You follow in spirit form.

Visualize a giant tree in the distance. The serpent draws you up high into the branches of the tree. All around you a beautiful river of stars drifts by. Imagine that you remove your green cord and dip it into the starry river. When you withdraw the cord it is glowing with starlight. You wind the cord back around your necklace.

You find yourself on a narrow ridge high on the wall of the cavern. The ridge forms a walkway down to the floor of the cavern. You walk carefully along the narrow path as you descend.

As you move along, the path suddenly ends. Suspended in front of you is a long knotted length of rope. There are seven widely separated knots that allow for your hands and feet to work their way down to the floor of the cavern. The rope hangs slightly out of your reach, and you must jump and catch hold of it. Visualize yourself taking this leap of faith.

Imagine yourself climbing down the rope ladder, taking note of each knot as you descend. At the end of the rope the floor of the cavern is only a couple of feet away. When you reach the bottom, you drop from the rope and gently land on the floor.

In the distance you see an altar with three candles burning. The serpent leads you over to it. When you arrive you notice that the candle on the left is black, the one in the middle is red, and the one on the right is white. In front of each candle is a gourd about the size of a soup bowl. Each one contains a measure of dried herb.

The gourd on the left is filled with peppermint. The middle one contains lavender, and the gourd on the right holds mandrake root. In this order, each bowl is marked with a symbol: on the left gourd is a star, the center gourd bears a caduceus, and the gourd on the right is marked with a spiral. The serpent instructs you to place your green cord in each gourd, one at a time, from left to right. Visualize this process.

The next phase is to imagine yourself coiling the green cord on the surface of your left hand, forming a spiral shape. Visualize the cord transforming into a solid and shiny black disk. As you look at the disk it seems to have great depth, as though you were peering into a deep well. After a few moments you see within the blackness of the disk a river of stars.

The serpent draws you back to the dangling rope of seven knots. Visualize leaping up to catch the rope, and then climbing back up the seven knots until you reach the ledge on the wall of the cavern. You swing on the rope and hop off onto the narrow walkway.

A large root is pressed against the wall of the cavern and leads upward. You climb the root in the dim light of the cavern. After a few moments you see what appears to be the blue surface water of a lake (as though you have been under water the entire time). The serpent then pulls you up through this membrane, and back up into the branches of the tree.

Imagine that you are sitting on a branch of this great old tree. You look again at the green cord and notice that is has retained the same starry night imagery. But now you can see the outline of the coiled cord tightly formed into a spiral shape. You pull on the outer edge of the cord and the spiral unravels into a long strand. The strand is colored black with sparkling stars running across its length. When you release the end of the cord it coils back into a spiral, and once again takes on the shape of a black disk with a river of stars.

The serpent nudges the disk with its nose and turns it over in your hand. The reverse side is entirely black, without any stars. It looks exactly like the darkness into which the roots of the great tree disappeared on your journey into the cavern. Visualize turning the coin over several times and take note that one side contains the river of stars and the other side does not.

It is time now to return from this journey. Visualize pulling the strand of cord free from its disk shape. Then imagine that you've tied one end of a rope to the tree branch. Visualize climbing down this rope and then swinging three times back and forth on the end of it. Using the rope you will return to the mortal world.

Visualize that on the final swing away from the tree you give a sharp tug on the rope. This releases the end tied to the tree, and you and the rope land safely back at the place where your journey began. This completes the phase of visualization and imagination.

Put the stone and white cord back between the candles. Take the green cord, form it into a spiral, and then touch it to each of the herbs on your work area. Moving from left to right, touch the peppermint and say the word *star*. Next touch the lavender and say *caduceus*, and end by touching the mandrake and say the word *spiral*.

With the cord still in a spiral shape, dip it into the water and submerge it for a few moments. During this period reflect back on everything you can remember about your journey. Try and recall every detail, what you thought about each event, and how you felt as you went along.

When you have finished, remove the cord from the water and hold it in your left hand. Rest this hand on the leaves of the ivy plant, and say these words:

Spirit of the ivy, I offer you this libation [squeeze some of the water from the cord onto the plant].

Spirit of the ivy, I ask that you entwine your binding energy around this cord, and hold therein the memory of my journey and its power. Make this cord an enchanted rope.

Take the cord and immerse it in the water. As you hold it under water, say these words:

River of stars and waters of the Underworld, your currents flow within this enchanted cord, and now also within me [remove the cord from the water, open your mouth and squeeze some water into it; then swallow the water].

Pour the remaining water onto the ivy plant, and then remove three of its leaves. Set them aside. Gather up the pinches of herb and place them in your carrying pouch. Tuck the three ivy leaves into the bag, and then place the green cord on top of them in the bag. This is now your personal power pouch containing your spirit cord.

Blow out the candles on your work area, and put everything away. This completes the alignment exercise. In future chapters you will be working more with this cord.

In the next chapter you will perform several pathworkings and encounter some beings that will aid you in the system this book presents. You will also be introduced to some mystical alignments that will help orient you to the work of cauldron retrieval.

We will end here with a simple blessing to be given over each cord individually. Place your palms above the cord and say:

> *By all the names of the Triformis Goddess; by all the elements of earth, air, fire, and water; and by the forces of the world above and the realm below; this cord is blessed and made sacred.*

Visualize a blue light enfolding the cord, and then picture it merging inside. When you work with the cords, always treat them with reverence as the sacred objects they are in nature. Possessing respect for the sacred, and working in partnership with sacredness will attract powerful allies to you. It will also open many portals as you work with the cauldron system.

SEVEN

SPIRIT JOURNEY

In this chapter, you will be introduced to a folkloric being known as the Crone of the Cottage. You will also encounter the meeting point between the worlds, which can serve as a doorway into other realms of existence. Both of these are key elements for working with the techniques presented in this book. It is through them that the journey to the Cauldron of Memory truly begins.

The story of the Crone is a very old one. Her tale is simple. As a young girl she is taken by the Faery race to their hidden realm and spends time in their company. Eventually she returns to the mortal world, but time in the land of the Fay is different from time in the mortal realm. Upon returning, the girl learns that everyone she has ever known is long since dead. She discovers that very little is familiar to her. The girl ends up living in a cottage in the woods, where she is aided and trained by the Faeries.

Over the course of time, she ages and crosses over to the Otherworld. Here she undergoes a great transformation and eventually returns to the mortal world in another form. She then takes her place as the mystical figure known as the Crone of the Cottage (a being neither mortal nor Faery). Here she serves as a *go-between* or *mediator* between humans and Faeries. Her wisdom and guidance is offered to all sincere seekers.

When you work with the Crone it is important to understand that this being is not mythical or imaginary. She actually exists as a *consciousness*, a sentient being capable of rendering great aid to you. The Crone is timeless and her essence flows through all the wise women that have ever lived and will ever live. In this light she may be regarded as an archetype.

Through the alignments in this book, and working with the Crone, you will be brought to the mystical crossroads. This is the legendary place that stands between the worlds. There is much to be gained in working with these alignments, because they trigger the flow of the momentum of the past.

In this section, and others in the book, you will be working with images from two related oracle decks: *The Well Worn Path* and *The Hidden Path*. The images in these decks were created to encapsulate the core essence of vital teachings that can be effectively used for pathworking. This is a relatively simple technique using a storyline that makes connections to inner planes awareness. Such connections create portals to altered states of consciousness. This, in turn, allows you to see and experience things that are usually veiled.

Before moving on to the practical work in this chapter, it is important to better understand the concept of the crossroads. In ancient times the liminal or "in-between" places were considered to possess unique power or influence. The intersection where three or four roads met was believed to be a connection to a realm outside of this world. In a similar manner, the inner frame of a doorway was considered to be neither inside nor outside of the house. Spirit forces were at work in such spaces, and therefore great care had to be taken. This concern is at the core of the origin of the custom of carrying the bride across the threshold.

The importance of roads applied not only to everyday life, but also to travels to distant places. Our ancestors believed that the dead also traveled on roads. Spirits that were unable to pass over into the Underworld found themselves at the crossroads.

In ancient times the goddess Enodia presided over roads, and another goddess known as Trivia presided over the joining of three roads. Here these goddesses served as aspects of the goddess Hecate who had dominion over the crossroads. Among the oldest practices associated with the crossroads was the placing of a tall wooden column. This was known as a *hekataion*.

The hekataion symbolized a mystical tree, which was its original form. This tree stood at the center of the crossroads and connected all worlds together. It also served as the portal between the world of the living and that of the dead. This is one of the reasons that lost souls came to the crossroads.

Since ancient times, the dead and the Underworld realm have been considered sources of oracle knowledge. In this light, the crossroads is the in-between point where communication is possible. Therefore, we will create an alignment to the crossroads in preparation for the journey to retrieve the Cauldron of Memory. It is one link in the memory-chain.

The sacred crossroads was typically located outside of the cities and towns. The vagabond class, which included sorcerers and witches, held their rituals and ceremonies at the crossroads. Here they gathered, without temples of their own, to lay claim to the freedom to worship as they pleased. The authorities and scholars of their time referred to this as an illicit religion, which means that it did not conform to the standards of officially accepted practices. In response, the "illicit class" people became, in effect, their own *society of the crossroads.*

The idea of crossroads work, depicted as noncompliant with the official view, is important because it is not constrained by any authorization, permission, or consent. The crossroads is a place of liberation from the expectations and the control of others. It is the setting in which personal fears and insecurities perish and are buried beneath the light of the moon. It is the moment of self-validation.

Preparing for Pathwork

In this section we will prepare for the pathwork exercises to follow in this chapter and others. Keep the Stone of Remembrance in your pouch and carry it with you at all times. This not only enhances the work, but also protects your mind, body, and spirit. When we work with nonmaterial world forces, we willingly open our psyche. Occult energy has a way of finding the weak spots in our emotional and mental makeup. This can result in the stimulation of psychological issues that are unresolved within us. Therefore it is essential to guard against such a mishap.

Required items:

• Your Stone of Remembrance

• White cord

• Bowl of fresh water

• Pen

• Paper

• Salt

To begin, pour some fresh water into a small bowl. Then add a pinch of salt. Mix this together with your finger. Dry off your finger and then lay the piece of paper in front of you. Using the pen, draw a circle (about the size of the palm of your hand). Next, inside the circle draw an equilateral cross. On top of the circle write the word "above." Beneath the circle write the word "below."

Looking now at the lines of the cross, place the letter "N" over the center of the top line. On the center line on the right, place the letter "E." For the bottom line you will mark the letter "S" in its center. On the left line, mark the letter "W" in the center.

On the center point where the lines intersect, place your white cord in a spiral shape. On top of the cord set your sacred stone. Spend a moment looking at the drawing, taking note that this symbol represents all your alignments to sacred space (within you and outside of you).

Now, pick up the stone and touch the word "above" and say the word out loud. Do the same for the word "below." Then, in a clockwise manner, use the stone to trace the circle from the letter "E" (the east) and back again. As you perform this, say "All around." Complete by touching each letter, and sounding the assigned tonal:

E: the vowel sound: Eeeeeeeeee

S: the vowel sound: Iiiiiiiiiii

W: the vowel sound: Ooooooooooo

N: the vowel sound: Aaaaaaaaaa

Above

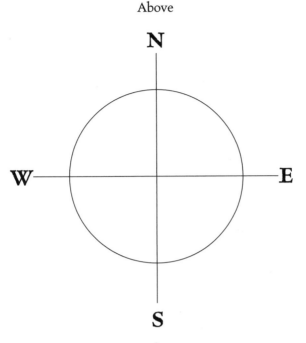

Below

Figure 3B: Pathwork Exercise

These tonals activate the elemental forces associated with the directions:

East: Air

South: Fire

West: Water

North: Earth

To complete this work, dip the stone in the water and anoint yourself: forehead, solar plexus, and genital area. Next, without touching the paper, use the stone to trace the entire imagery you drew. This means that you will repeat the entire exercise again (including the tonals and anointing yourself with the water).

Place the paper on your lap. End with these words spoken over the stone and the drawing:

I call upon the power of elemental earth to stabilize and fortify all pro-
cesses. I call upon the elemental power of air to balance my thoughts. I
call upon the elemental power of fire to transform negative into positive.
I call upon the elemental power of water to purify. I call upon the power
of elemental earth to stabilize and fortify all processes.

Once completed, place the stone and the cord back in your pouch and keep it on your person while you work.

End by invoking Hermes to accompany you on your pathworking venture (see chapter eight for invocation). Now you are ready to move on to the first set of pathwork adventures in succession. It is recommended that you audio record the pathwork journeys and play them back. Ideally, have someone other than yourself speaking, but if this is not practical for your situation then use your own voice. In any case, for now just read the pathwork stories to yourself, and then later on you can use the audio to perform the pathwork alignments.

Pathwork: Meeting the Crone of the Cottage

In this section you will be focusing on the symbolism and imagery of the Crone card. Take a few moments to study what the card depicts. Take note of the elderly woman at her desk. She is writing her knowledge and wisdom onto the pages of a journal.

The Crone sits in her warm cottage, surrounded by the things she has collected over the years. Books are tucked together on a shelf above her. Next to the books is the Crone's pet raven, which brings her messages and guards her domain. A crystal ball also sits on the shelf, and through this she sees into other worlds.

Behind her in the corner of the room is an old staff, which accompanies her when she ventures out into the woods. It is a branch from the sacred tree that stands between the worlds. Hanging on the wall are the dried herbs that she collects from field and forest. They keep her attuned with the plant kingdom, for the Crone is the healer, potion maker, and seer. On the table a candle is set, giving its light to the Crone. She is the Keeper of the Flame, one who is an initiate of the Old Ways of our ancestors. In her is the memory ensuring that nothing is ever forgotten.

CRONE

Now that you have this alignment to the Crone, it is time to encounter her on your pathwork journey. As the following story unfolds, visualize each detail. Take your time with the individual imagery before moving on with the story. If you do so you will notice that things appear during the journey that are not actually mentioned in the story. These are important, so pay attention to them.

Do not try to force anything to happen or appear. Enjoy what is generated. You cannot fail, because you are not in control. Therefore do not enter into this pathworking with any expectations. Simply allow it to be whatever you experience. Let us begin.

Imagine yourself walking down a country road that leads into the woods. It is almost twilight as the sun is slipping into the distant horizon. Your walk takes you closer to the trees, and before long you pass into the forest. Continue walking deeper in the forest.

You hear the sound of a raven above, and looking up you see it sitting on a branch. In its talons is a stone. When you decide to move on, you find that the road has disappeared and you are surrounded by thick woods all around you. This is not the place where you stopped when the raven called out.

You look back up at the branch. The raven is still there, and it drops the stone at your feet. You pick it up and see that the stone has a smooth hole worn completely through its center. Curious, you hold it up to your left eye and look through the hole. In front of you now appears the pathway.

Relieved, you continue walking along the road leading through the woods. All around you is the beauty of this natural setting. Up ahead and just off to the left side of the road you notice a cottage. It draws you in some mystical way and you move up the road toward the cottage.

As you arrive at the cottage, you note that there is a light in the window. Smoke rises from the chimney. Through the window you see the kind face of the Crone smiling at you. A wave of her hand bids you enter.

You go to the door, which she opens to greet you. You follow her inside. She walks over to her writing desk and sits. You join her at the desk. The Crone gently lays her hand on top of yours, looks into your eyes, and says: "*So, let's see, who do we have here?*"

As her eyes seemed locked upon yours, you quickly get the feeling that she is seeing more than just your face. You realize that the eyes of the Crone are looking into your soul. Here she sees all that you have seen and experienced. Through you, the Crone also views the lives of everyone in your lineage, back to the very beginning. Within a few moments she smiles, sits back, and says: "*Oh, yes, I know you; I remember you very well.*"

The Crone pats your hand, rises, and says she has something you need to see. "*Come along,*" she says, and you follow her out of the cottage, onto the road in front of her home. "*It's just a little ways on.*" She winks and the two of you set off down the trail.

It is now early evening; the full moon is clearing the tree tops and shedding light on the path. Up in the distance you notice a glow on the ground in the center of the road. The Crone places her hand on your back, and points to the area with her the other hand. "*There it is,*" she says, and her face reflects a great reverence for the moment.

You ask, "*There is what?*" and the answer comes back "*The crossroads, of course.*"

Pathwork: The Crossroads

In this section we will be working with the imagery of the crossroads card. Examine each item in the picture. Let them wash over you as you spend a few moments with each item.

Essentially, the card depicts the hekataion pole with the symbol of Hecate hanging above the masks, symbolizing the three-fold-labyrinth of her mysteries. The masks represent Hecate's triformis nature as the Lady above, center, and below (the Three Worlds). A key is shown suspended on the pole, and is symbolic of the fact that the hidden mysteries can be open or closed to us at the crossroads, for only the sincere seeker can enter and pass through.

On the card are thirteen candles, which symbolize the lunar cycle of the year. This connects the theme to the Goddess of the Crossroads, who is also the Goddess of the Moon. Nine pomegranates appear at the base of the hekataion as offerings to the Goddess of the Crossroads. Such offerings are sacred to the Underworld, and through this alignment we can draw upon the oracle forces they represent.

Now you are ready to begin this pathwork. Imagine yourself standing in front of the crossroads. The dark sacred night forms a dome above you. Visualize the stars twinkling above in the night sky. Spend a moment thinking about this seemingly endless expansion, and then reflect on the idea that all of this is under the domain of the Great Goddess.

You look at the hekataion before you and see three masks attached to it. The faces are alive and you see them looking in all directions. You realize that this represents the limitless expansion of the starry sky above, for the stars are the watchers in the night. Next you notice a single key hanging from a cord tied to the pole.

The key seems to gently draw your left hand to it, and so you reach out and touch the key by pressing your open palm against it (*spend a few moments with this visualization before proceeding*).

With your palm against the key, you feel a sensation. Allow this to continue for a few moments, and then bring your hand to rest at your side. Now your attention is drawn to the symbol above the three masks. It is the symbol known as the Wheel of Hecate. You gaze at it for a few

THE CROSSROADS

moments, and then you become aware that your left palm is tingling. You look at it and find that an image of the key has appeared on your palm.

As you look at your hand, the image of the key transforms into the symbol of Hecate. You look back at the hekataion and there in place of Hecate's symbol is the image of your open hand with the key on the center of your palm. The images exchange places three times, and then all is as it was before (*spend a few moments visualizing this process*).

Your attention is now drawn to the pomegranates on the ground. You kneel down to see them more closely. A soft wind moves and the candle flames bend as the wind passes across them. The wind seems like it must have been the breath of life, because you now notice that faces rise up from within the fruit, press against the skin to form a mask covering, and then recede back again (*visualize this for a few moments*). These are your ancestors, sensing your presence at the crossroads.

You stand back up again, facing the hekataion. Behind it you notice that the road divides with one fork to the left and the other to the right. There are choices that lie ahead. Chose the path on the right and prepare for a journey (*you can repeat the journey using the left fork in the road at a later time*).

Pathwork: Oak, Ash, and Thorn

In this section you will be focusing on the symbolism and imagery of the Oak, Ash, and Thorn. Take a few moments to study what the card depicts. Give special note to the cluster formed by the three trees.

The card depicts an ash tree (left) and an oak tree (right) with a hawthorn tree in the center. Notice that the hawthorn tree is blocking the opening between the ash and oak. The upper branches of the ash and oak form an archway, suggesting the presence of a portal to another realm beyond. From this vantage point spirits in the foliage watch all who approach.

The oak, ash, and hawthorn trees are legendary guardians that bar the way into the Otherworld. The oak and ash stand as the portals at the threshold. The hawthorn, with its sharp spikes, guards against easy access. Between the ash and the oak is the in-between place, which is neither in this world nor in the next. It is a place of magic where anything is possible.

Let's begin the journey. You are walking along the path leading from the crossroads. The path takes you to a group of three trees and seemingly comes to an end. You look at the trees and notice the one in the center has thorns on its branches. Some force seems to prevent you from walking around the tree.

In the overhead branches of the trees appear the faces of many forest spirits. Each one watches you closely. You sense a danger here as these spirits are fierce guardians. While being watched, you hear a groaning sound and you notice that the branches of the oak and ash tree move together. Their branches interlock like fingers joined together.

You feel a tingling sensation in the palm of your left hand. Looking down, you notice the symbol of the key reappearing on your hand. You look at the symbol, and once again it transforms back and forth from the key to the symbol of Hecate. It does this three times and then remains the symbol of the key (*spend a few moments with this imagery*).

OAK, ASH AND THORN

Seeing this as a sign, you display the key symbol to the tree. You hear the sound of the wind passing through the leaves on the trees. Faint whispers arise from the spirits on the tree branches. A soft glow surrounds the center tree. You hold your hand in place, and now the branches of this tree part to allow you safe passage (*spend a few moments visualizing this event*).

These pathwork exercises complete the practical work for this chapter. In the next chapter you will be presented with more exercises to lead you into inner planes contact. You will also encounter allies to assist you. These are all preparations for the task of retrieving the hidden Cauldron of Memory.

EIGHT

OTHERWORLD CONTACTS

For countless centuries people have believed in spirits, entities, and beings that belong to another world. Connected to this is the idea of a world outside of the material realm. Among the classic models is the realm of the Elven or Faery race. This is often referred to as the Otherworld.

In myth and legend we find tales in which humans and Faeries interact. Among the earliest stories, the relationship is primarily cordial and peaceful. In later tales, the Faeries are depicted as easy to offend, and great care must be taken to ensure goodwill. With the dawning of the Christian era, the Faeries are portrayed as mischievous and dangerous. Stories tell of the Faeries kidnapping humans, swapping babies for changelings, and bringing harm or disease through the use of magical darts. But these are intentionally distorted portrayals designed to vilify and therefore discourage interest in pre-Christian beliefs and practices.

Today there is a rapidly rising interest in Faery traditions. This is due, in part, to contact from the Otherworld. All dimensions of existence share a resonance that connects them together through the emanation of energy. Each world is, in effect, influenced by the others. Unfortunately our material world is being adversely affected by human activity, which is polluting the atmosphere and destroying natural resources at an alarming rate. As a result, the other worlds are receiving currents of destructive energy from the material realm.

In response to what is being generated, we are now seeing a return of visitations and communications from inter-dimensional beings. These beings were known by many names in ancient times. Among the most influential are the Elven or Faery beings. It should be noted, however, that these are not the cute little winged creatures of popular fairy tales.

The beings that are making contact with humans today are a very ancient race. They are wise, skillful, and very powerful. Long ago they withdrew from direct human contact because our primitive behavior was both dangerous and abrasive to these advanced beings. For ages they were content to leave us alone until our technology made that position no longer feasible.

In the 1960s, people experimented with mind-expanding drugs and various methods of obtaining altered states of consciousness. A renewed interest in astrology and the occult arts rose within society. An anti-war or peace movement swept across the planet. This energy intrigued beings from the Otherworld and they were drawn back to the material realm through the old portals. In the following decades we saw religions and magical systems such as Wicca and Witchcraft come into full light.

In the midst of this arose the New Age movement, which incorporated a variety of beliefs and practices from multiple cultures. Groups and individuals believing in visitations from other planets were added to the movement. The New Age movement quickly became an all-you-can-eat buffet of diverse beliefs and practices. This seems to have renewed interaction between humans and nonhumans in beneficial and hopeful ways.

For the purposes of this book we will be working with Elven contacts. The Elven are, in the view of this work, a high order of Faery beings. They dwell on a mystical island in the west. In the center of the island is a castle. It can sometimes be seen by humans just as the sun sets on the horizon.

Contact with the Elven is made through several pathworkings provided in this chapter. For imagery we will be using the Faery Door, the Kindred, and the Otherworld cards. These are the final pathworkings needed before finally descending to retrieve the Cauldron of Memory. We will do this in the next chapter. But for now we must take the last steps of preparation. Each of the following pathworkings are components of a larger one. Therefore work with each in succession.

Before beginning the following pathworkings, place a small opened container of honey next to you. You will encounter certain entities in one of the journeys, and the honey will ensure the most beneficial outcome.

Pathwork: The Faery Door

This exercise picks up where you left off with the Oak, Ash, and Thorn pathworking in the previous chapter. Take a moment to recall standing before the thorn tree, and remember it parting to allow you passage. With this in mind, you are ready to begin.

Study the image of the Faery Door card for a few moments. Next, imagine yourself standing in front of a hawthorn tree. It has parted its branches and lowered them to allow you to step over the foliage. In front of you there stands an old wooden door set in the midst of an oak and ash tree.

On the door is the triformis symbol that denotes the presence of mystical and magic forms of energy. This energy is always associated with magic and transformation. Looking at the door, you notice that the knob is shaped like an apple. The apple is the fruit of the Otherworld and is sacred to the Faery race. As you look at the door you realize it is slightly open. A silvery light seeps through and beckons you to enter.

You take the knob into your right hand and gently push to enter through the open door. As you enter, it is as though you penetrate through a veil of light. This light is the only thing your eyes can see for a moment. Now the door closes behind you and the silvery light fades away.

You find yourself standing in a beautiful meadow. It is summertime and everything is in full bloom. Passing through the center of the meadow is a well worn path leading off into the distance and disappearing into a forest.

FAERY DOOR

You walk along the path on your way to the woods. All around are your favorite flowers, herbs, and other plants. The air is fragrant, the sun is warm in the blue sky, and it brings to you memories of carefree summer days in your youth.

You are now approaching the forest. The trees in this forest are all the magical and mythical ones of ancient myth and legend. The stories of Bards, the tales of enchantments, all fairy tales, and all legends of woodland heroes and spirits are set in areas of this magical realm.

The well worn path that took you to the forests now leads you into the woods. You are walking along the trail, passing deeper into the woods. Sunlight falls filtered through the branches. In the trees various birds look down upon you. You hear stirring sounds in the brush around you. You continue walking through the woods.

Ahead in the distance you can make out a clearing in the woods. As you draw nearer, you notice a gigantic and ancient tree. It curves upward, bending in several places much like the movement of a snake.

You are now standing in front of this tree. On each bend of the tree trunk a rustic cottage has been constructed. Throughout time the trunk of the old tree has grafted itself onto the back of each building. It now seems as though the cottages have grown from the tree.

As you study the structures, it is clear that these homes are not abandoned. You can hear the sound of movement and of voices coming from the cottages. Suddenly you hear a buzzing sound like a hive of bees all around you. Before you can react to this sound, it changes into tiny chimes. The melody is enchanting. You feel a presence behind you. You are not alone as you stand before the ancient tree.

Pathwork: The Kindred

Study the imagery on this card. Starting from the figure on the top left side, move clockwise as you take note of each character. The crowns denote that these Elven beings hold a particular office or standing within the Faery community.

The first male figure is the Seer, one who can pierce the veil between past, present, and future. The female beside him is the Magician; she directs the forces of transformation. Next in order is the Bard who is the keeper and guardian of sacred knowledge and wisdom. The final female figure is the Envisioner. She can materialize anything that her inner mind conceives; she is the weaver and shaper of the inner planes. Together this Elven fellowship preserves the natural order, envisions the future, sees all ends, and transforms reality for the good of all beings.

Begin your pathworking by recalling the sound of wind chimes from the previous exercise. Imagine yourself back at the ancient tree. You are aware of a presence behind you, and as you turn, there are four Elven beings who greet you. They do not speak, smile, nor extend a hand, but you correctly sense that you are welcome and safe here. Spend a few moments and wait to see what transpires between you and these Elven beings.

When you are ready to move on, imagine that the Seer points to the base of the trunk of the gigantic tree. The Magician passes her hand across your eyes. You suddenly see an opening in the trunk of the

THE KINDRED

tree—a great hollow with a tunnel passageway into the tree. The Bard explains that this is a Faery Door that leads into an enchanted kingdom. He then takes out a small flute and plays three single notes, which he repeats three times. Next, the Envisoner touches your forehead with her fingertips, and for a moment you feel as though you may pass into a sleep.

Imagine that you enter the hollow and begin walking down a long tunnel. The Elven beings accompany you. The tunnel continues on in a straight path. After a few moments you see some light, which indicates an opening at the end of the tunnel. You continue to walk forward.

You have now reached the end of the tunnel. You pass through on to an embankment. A few feet ahead of you is a large hedge with an archway cut through its center. As you approach the arch, a mist forms inside it. It quickly becomes so thick you cannot see what is on the other side. Your Elven companions encourage you to pass through the mist.

Imagine yourself walking in a thick mist that completely envelops you. It takes on an air of magic and the idea occurs to you that if you could project an image into the mist, the object would surely manifest. You hear one of the Elven speak, but you cannot understand the language. When the words cease, the mist begins to thin. It continues to thin until you find yourself standing on an embankment. It slopes gently down to the shores of a great lake.

Pathwork: The Otherworld

Study the imagery on the Otherworld card. This card depicts the portal to the Otherworld, which is veiled by a heavy mist. Beyond the parted mist is the shore of the Otherworld, as seen from the lake. In the center of the island is a castle. This castle is featured in various tales of cauldron quests and mystical journeys.

The woman in the boat is the Lady of the Lake, a legendary figure associated with mystical realms. Above her fly three swans, which are symbols of Faery encounters and magical events.

Begin this pathworking by recalling the gentle slope leading down to the lake. Picture yourself walking down to the shore. As you approach, a boat materializes in front of you. Standing in it is a woman of great mystery. She gestures to you to enter the boat. You step into it and feel it rock gently beneath your feet on the water.

The boat moves from the shore and you feel yourself sway slightly backward from the momentum. Ahead of you on the water is a swirling mist that blocks the sight of anything other than itself. The woman raises her hand and hums an ancient melody. The mist parts to receive the boat, and in the distance you see an island with white sand and a castle rising in its midst.

You can feel the boat gliding across the water as the island draws nearer. You now feel its motion slowing, and then the boat slides up against the shore. You rock forward slightly as the boat touches home. The woman motions for you to leave the boat and step onto the island.

You leave the boat and step onto the shore. You feel a presence beside you and turn to see the Kindred. They greet you and then

OTHERWORLD

gesture for you to follow them as they move off to the right. You follow behind them.

As you walk, to the left of you is the castle sitting upon a hill. The Kindred turn and begin to move along a path leading up the hill. You walk with them heading up the hillside along the road. You become aware of the sound of gentle wind chimes.

You are now approaching the lowered drawbridge to the castle. You follow the Kindred across it, and you can hear the sound of feet walking on the wooden planks. It sounds almost hollow as you walk along the suspended bridge. Ahead of you is the opening to the castle.

You follow the Kindred into the castle. Inside to the right is a large wooden door. Marked on the center is the symbol of a cornucopia. The Kindred open the door and you follow them inside. You are now in a large hall.

In the center of the hall is a throne. All along the walls of the chamber, rich purple curtains hang from floor to ceiling. The Kindred gesture to you, instructing you to sit on the throne. You move to the chair and sit down.

To your right you notice the movement of a purple curtain. From behind it appear nine lovely Faery women wearing white gowns and carrying a cauldron. They bring the cauldron over and set it in front of you. Each woman then draws a small vial from her gown and pours the liquid contents into the cauldron.

You look down inside the cauldron to see that the liguid has formed a dark mirror. For a moment you see yourself reflected on the surface, but this fades away quickly and only the blackness remains. You hear one of the maids say, "*Look here, this is yours.*"

You look at the dark surface inside the cauldron and something appears there. Spend a few moments with this visualization, but don't force it; let it come of its own accord (once you see or sense what the cauldron offers, remember the image or the feeling). Retrieve this from the cauldron with your left hand.

The nine maidens lift the cauldron and move off, disappearing behind the purple curtain. The Kindred gesture for you to rise and follow them. You leave the throne behind and walk out of the chamber with the Kindred. Outside of the door the Kindred turn to the left and then begin crossing the drawbridge back to the shore.

You follow them across the bridge. At the end you begin moving down the path as it descends the hill. Visualize yourself moving away from the castle and down the slope. Spend a few moments with this step.

Mentally see yourself at the bottom of the hill. The Kindred turn right along the shoreline, and you follow them. You are heading back to the location where you left the boat. Spend a few moments visualizing yourself moving along the shore.

To your left, on the water of the lake, you see the boat with the woman waiting for you. You have now returned to the point at which you first made contact with the island. You can return anytime you wish by following the series of pathworking steps in this chapter.

It is now time to record what you saw in the cauldron. Draw it on a piece of paper or obtain a picture of it from some source. If you didn't see anything in the cauldron, then you have two choices. You can draw a simple spiral or make a circle and color it in thoroughly with black ink or pencil. You will keep the drawing tucked into the pouch that contains your Stone of Remembrance, so keep this in mind when considering the size of your copy.

Pathwork: The Way of Return

The pathworkings in this chapter have opened inner planes gateways. Each of these lead to specific states of consciousness that are activated by the images in the storyline. These energies carry *momentum of the past* and *morphic resonance*. Therefore, like all pathworkings, you must deactivate them and resume your everyday mode of consciousness. We all need to operate from the mode of consciousness that is pertinent to the moment in which we find or place ourselves.

To temporarily shut down the altered states of consciousness you will need to leave the realm of each pathworking in the order in which you encountered it. Therefore you now move from the Otherworld back to the Kindred (at the gigantic tree) and then finally return through the Faery Door.

To begin the way of return, picture yourself climbing back into the boat with the Lady of the Lake figure. The boat moves backward away from the shore, and you rock forward in response to the movement. The boat then turns to the right and begins gliding back across the lake.

As you move along the lake you are now aware that a swirling mist is pouring in all around you. It quickly blocks out anything other than itself. Spend a few moments imagining being completely engulfed in the mist.

Visualize the mist fading away, and in the distance is the shore from which you departed to the Otherworld island. The boat glides gently along the water. You feel it begin to slow, and then it slides into the shore. Your body sways forward with the gentle impact. You are now back from the Otherworld island.

You step from the boat and give thanks to the Lady of the Lake. Ahead of you is a path leading up the embankment. You move up the gentle slope and approach the hedge with the archway cut through its center. As you pass through the opening, a soft mist pours down over your body from head to toe. You step through to the other side of the hedge.

Just a few steps away is the tunnel leading back to the gigantic tree. You enter it and begin walking. Spend a few moments in this visualization. Walking along through the tunnel, you now see some light at its end. Just a few steps further, and then you exit the tunnel.

You are now standing with your back to the gigantic tree. Turn around and face it, and take note of the shape of the tree (seeing its snake-like bends and the old cottage nestled in each one). As you look at the tree you hear a sound like the buzzing of bees. It quickly changes to the sound of melodious wind chimes. You turn around to find the Kindred standing before you.

You give thanks to the Kindred for all they have done for you. They smile warmly, but do not speak, and you know that you are welcome to return to them whenever you wish. There are gifts that were given you through the touch of the Kindred, and these will serve you well in the future.

You begin walking back through the woods. It is later in the day than when you entered. You hear again the sounds of birds and animals as you walk along. Spend a few moments walking back through the woods.

You come now to the end of the forest. Ahead is the meadow from which you first entered the woods. You are now walking along the well worn path leading through the center of the meadow. All around you are your favorite flowers, herbs, and plants. You continue walking.

Up ahead you notice a vast wall of fog. As you approach it you see an old wooden door in the center. On the door is a copper replica of a human skull. Surrounding it are jewels in a circle around the skull. The door knob is shaped like a spiral colored gold and silver.

You open the door and step through. You are now standing in the middle of three trees, an oak, ash, and a hawthorn. The door closes behind you. You look back and there is no door to be seen; all you can see is the forest where you first encountered the three trees.

Ahead of you, leading out of the woods, is a narrow pathway. You begin walking along, following it out of the woods. A short distance ahead, you see a clearing. As you approach it, you see the hekataion pole in the center of the crossroads. Spend a few moments with this imagery.

It is time to move on. You take the path on the left and begin the final steps of your long journey home. You walk along the path, and up ahead a swirling column of mist moves toward you on the road. You take three steps forward when the mist engulfs you. Spend a few moments visualizing the surrounding mist.

The mist dissolves away and the path is clear. You walk along the road and up ahead on the right you see the cottage of the Crone. There is a light coming from the window and smoke rises from the chimney. You come to the front of the cottage. In the window is the smiling face of the Crone.

The Crone winks and gestures for you to continue walking back homeward along the path. You give her a nod of respect, and you sense that you are welcome to return to the cottage any time you wish.

Now you are ready to complete this pathworking. Become aware of the physical presence of the book you are reading. Tap the floor several times with your feet. Take notice of any sounds around you. Now take in three deep breaths, exhaling slowly after each one. End by clapping your hands sharply three times. Have a small snack and something to drink. Do not skip this final step.

Working with Elven Contacts

Before moving on to the next chapter you will need to perform a couple of pathworking alignments. These will help you strengthen the relationship with your ally spirits. These beings can aid you in understanding what you will experience through the system in this book. They can also serve as personal teachers so that you may move forward after working with this book.

You can read books by various authors that will describe Elven or Faery beings and provide information about them. I am not going to do this here as I prefer to leave it to these beings to inform you directly. I regard this as part of the teaching process when working with these entities. Therefore, in this section we will look at ways of making contact and establishing rapport.

It should be noted that it is not uncommon for the initial contacts with the Elven/Faery to be somewhat unsettling. The Elven are not the beings of children's fairy tales. There is no inherent danger, but you may find the first couple of meetings to be somewhat challenging. In one of my first encounters, a Faery woman appeared to me as a five-foot-tall tarantula! She eventually transformed into a beautiful young black woman, which I must admit was quite a relief.

One old tradition of meeting the Elven involves going to the crossroads. In northern European traditions, the crossroads is the meeting of four intersecting roads. Each of these roads is associated with one of the four elements in occult tradition: North (earth), East (air), South (fire) and West (water). Some traditions also incorporate the sacred directions of above and below into the system of correspondences.

In southern Europe we know that the crossroads was defined in the earliest written accounts as being the place where three roads met. The number three has long been associated with mystical themes. One example is the idea of the Three Fates and another concept is the "triangle of manifestation," which represents the three required components for anything to materialize. These are: time (when something comes into existence), space (where something comes into existence), and energy (what moves something toward existence).

To begin working the Elven contacts, we will be using the Crossroads card from the *Well Worn Path* divination deck. This image depicts three roads. If you wish instead to work with the four-road concept you can draw an equilateral cross on a piece of paper. Place the Crossroads card on the center of your drawing (making sure that the arms of the cross are long enough to extend out from the card so you can see them clearly).

Position yourself comfortably. Imagine the sky above you, first the day sky and then the night. Mentally acknowledge the firm ground beneath you. Next, imagine the hollow space of the world deep beneath

THE CROSSROADS

you, the very center of the earth. Now become aware of the directional points around you: north, east, south, and west. While imagining these directions, make the associated sounds in sequence:

Above: Ah-oom

East: Eeeeee

South: Iiiiii

West: Ooooooo

North: Aaaaaa

Below: Oom-ah

Now visualize a swirling sphere of blue light in front of you. Direct your voice into the light and make this connected chain of sounds: Ah-oom-eeee-iiii-oooo-aaaa-oom-aah.

As the last sound begins to fade, lower both hands (palms facing down) just above the crossroads card (almost touching it). Then visualize the blue light entering the card and being part of it.

The next step is to picture yourself standing at the crossroads. In your mind's eye see the hekataion pole. Once clearly pictured, visualize the blue light glowing in a large sphere in front of the pole. Spend a few moments with this imagery.

While your image of the blue sphere is still clear, visualize an Elven/Faery being stepping out of the light. Allow this being to take on the appearance of its choice. Do not anticipate, direct, or modify its appearance. In time it may change its form as it continues to work with you; in fact, this is very likely. For now, just go with the experience.

Once the Elven/Faery has taken form, greet it with respect. In most cases the Elven/Faery being will then initiate communication. However, if he or she is silent, then you can and should ask questions. Do not spend time in idle chatter nor waste time with small matters. Above all, be honest and forthright. Dishonesty or deception is not tolerated by Elven/Faery beings, not even in the slightest degree. They can read your energy and are never wrong in their discernment.

Often the Elven/Faery will communicate to you in images of projected thought. Other times you will hear an internal voice. In any case, remain receptive and listen closely. After each session write down everything as best you remember. Keep a journal specifically for this work.

When you first begin working with any unknown entity, do not accept any food or drink from them (nor any gift). Thank the entity, but add that you do not feel *worthy* to accept at this time. This simply means that you decline with no offense intended. It doesn't mean that you actually have no worth. However the use of the term is good public relations for the setting.

After a few more encounters you can feel safe to receive what the Elven/Faery offer to you (but never do so if your intuition makes you sense trouble or danger). It is very unlikely that this will happen to you in these pathworkings, but I would be remiss not to advise you of the possibilities. At the core of this all, we are talking about character (yours and that of the Elven/Faery). Everything you encounter is a reaction to your personal vibration. One of the goals of pathworking with the Elven/Faery is to spiritually raise and transform that vibration in beneficial ways for all concerned.

Once you have developed a good working relationship with your allies, you can then move on to guided encounters within other realms. These are likely to place you in challenging situations. Spiritual enlightenment is about achieving a balance between light and dark, positive and negative, active and receptive. If all of your experiences are pleasant, effortless, and lighthearted, then you have never truly moved beyond the confines of your own imagination.

When you are ready to finish working with the allies, simply return to the crossroads imagery. See the blue light forming into a sphere. Thank the ally for working with you by saying words like this:

> I thank you for your attendance and respectfully depart now as you return to your own realm. May there always be peace between us.

Visualize the Elven/Faery moving into the blue light and disappearing. Next, visualize the blue sphere expanding and dissolving away, returning its composition back into the directions: above, north, east, south, west, and below.

Arrange a schedule of working with the allies at least once a month. You can recall the same Elven/Faery each time at the crossroads, or be receptive to another appearance manifesting. In time you will have more than one ally in any case. Remember not to misuse the allies by needlessly calling upon them for small matters that you can handle yourself.

Do not ask the allies to perform things like healing. It is better to state the problem and let the Elven/Faery deal with the matter at hand as they deem appropriate. The allies are not servants, they are companions and guides. One exception to the rule is in time of danger. They can and should be called upon for protection on the inner planes.

Working with Hermes

One of the safeguards I have built into this system incorporates calling on the god Hermes as a companion, escort, and guardian. He has counterparts in other European systems if you prefer to use something other than an Aegean-Mediterranean model. One example is the Celtic god known as Lugh. You can research others in mythology books or on the Internet. Search using the name Mercury as well as Hermes (Mercury is the Roman name). However, my advice is to work with Hermes.

In this section we will construct a tool known as the herald's wand. It will be used as a ritual tool to aid in the retrieval of ancestral memory in the cauldron pathworking techniques described in this chapter. You will be using it primarily to help with interpreting the communication coming from the inner Cauldron of Memory.

As mentioned in previous chapters, Hermes is an escort of souls into the Afterlife realms. He wears a helmet that renders him invisible, which means that it allows him to travel in spirit form. This theme also applies to the legendary Stone of Remembrance that possessed the power of invisibility in its associated tales. This stone appears in the Mabinogion legends and other mythic tales where it bestows a number of magical gifts.

Before moving on to the practical work, it is beneficial to know more about Hermes, his nature, and abilities. In mythology he is the son of Zeus and Maia. His mother was one of the seven maidens who were transformed into the seven stars that make up the constellation Pleiades.

In her legends, Maia is described as a shy goddess who avoided the company of other deities. She lived in a shadowy cave, which is where Zeus mated with her while his wife Hera was asleep on Mount Olympus. Hermes was born in the cave inhabited by Maia. The association with the cave is a chthonic symbol connecting Maia and Hermes with the Underworld.

Maia is associated with the month of May (when the Pleiades rise) and with the theme of "Mother Goddess" due to her connection with growth and the plant kingdom. In ancient Rome the date of May 15 was established as her festival day (along with Mercury/Hermes). In Rome,

Maia was also known as Majesta (a goddess associated with oaths and honor).

In myth and legend Hermes is associated with three virgins who take on the form of bee-maidens known as the Thryai or Thryae. In their mythos they are described as "holy ones" and virgins with wings, whose heads are dusted with white barley meal. They are teachers of divination and feed on honey. When given honey, they respond with accurate forecasts, but when denied honey their accounts are unreliable (and in some tales they are intentionally deceiving). Some commentators believe the Thryai are the classic Three Fates in an archaic form.

One of the earliest depictions of Hermes is as a god that protected travelers. As a god of the roads, this aspect comes as no surprise. In addition to this aspect of Hermes, we are also interested in him as a guide for souls crossing to and from the world of the living. In this regard we invoke or evoke his aid when working with various mental journeys into the inner planes (the most important of which are presented in chapter nine).

When working with Hermes, take note that his sacred day is Wednesday; therefore this is a good day for enlisting his aid. For ritual item correspondences, you can incorporate agate stones, the herbs known as rosemary and lavender, and the color yellow. With these items you can assemble an alignment pouch to wear when calling upon Hermes or simply wishing to enhance your aura with his energy. If using a pouch for this purpose, add a Mercury dime as a power alignment.

Making the Herald's Wand

To construct the herald's wand, you will need a dowel. I prefer wood because it is lighter than metal and therefore easier to wield. A good length to work with is twelve inches. You will also need some white paint, two ribbons (one red, one black), and some glue or something else to adhere the ribbons onto the dowel. In addition you will need a black permanent marker pen to draw symbols on the wand. Make sure the white paint is compatible with the marker pen.

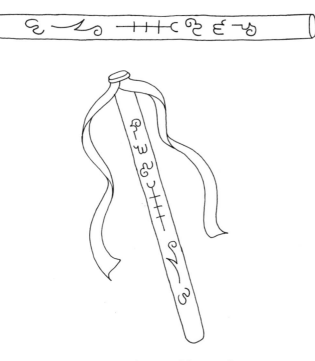

Figure 4: The Herald's Wand

Begin by painting the wand white, and then allow it to dry thoroughly before proceeding. Once it is dry, mark the symbols as shown in the illustration. These are ritual symbols that correspond to the planetary nature of the planet Mercury. Therefore, you will work with the higher or celestial nature of Hermes when you use the ritual tool.

With the tool painted and marked, you can then add the ribbons. Adhere them to the top of the wand, one on each side. Attach only the ends of the ribbons to the wand. The ribbons should hang freely from the top. Once the wand is completed, consecrate it with the following invocation:

By the power of the four elements of creation, and by the forces at the crossroads. I consecrate this wand to be a tool of the god Hermes. I call upon this wand to assist me in unraveling the mysteries presented to my mind and to help reveal that which is hidden or obscured.

Hold the wand upright, move it slowly in a clockwise direction, and sound out each elemental tonal using the following invocation as you visualize the energy passing into the wand:

Air, bestow upon this wand the ability to discern [make the vowel sound Eeee].

Fire, bestow upon this wand the ability to transform the misshapen into its original form [make the vowel sound Iiii].

Water, bestow upon this wand the ability to wash away the sediment and reveal what is covered beneath [make the vowel sound Oooo].

Earth, bestow upon this wand the ability to reveal the true foundations (make the vowel sound Aaaa).

Stop moving the wand clockwise, and bring it to rest. Hold it outward in the manner of presenting it, and say these words:

By the power of the four elements, and in the name of Hermes, I declare this tool to be the herald's wand, a device to correctly interpret whatever I meditate upon.

Now, begin moving the wand counterclockwise as you say the following words:

By the power of the four elements, and in the name of Hermes, this wand will disperse all falsehood, trickery, and deception whenever called upon to do so.

Stop moving the wand counterclockwise, and bring it to rest. When not in use, keep the wand put away or wrapped in a cloth. You will be using the wand when working the cauldron exercise so you will want to have it with you at such times. Use the following invocation to Hermes each time you employ the wand to aid any cauldron exercise or path-working journey.

The Invocation of Hermes

Hermes, come to me, you who wield influence over the four sacred directions, the in-between places, and the spaces above and below. Thee I invoke; come to me in favorable aspect, you who no magic can enchant or control. Come unto me, Lord Hermes, you of many names, who knows the secrets both beneath the poles of heaven and underneath the earth! Preserve me from all deceits and enchantments of every kind. Grant me success and victory in all my quests.

Now that you have reached the end of this chapter you are prepared to begin your inner quest for the Cauldron of Memory.

NINE

THE CAULDRON WITHIN

The ancient philosopher Marcus Cicero once stated that the life of the dead is placed in the memory of the living. This quote speaks to the heart of what is presented in this chapter. It is part of the mystery teachings that each new generation carries the voices of its forbearers throughout time.

In modern Wiccan belief and some other pagan traditions we find a teaching that the soul can reincarnate within a specific bloodline. Through this it can "meet, know, and remember" those who were loved in a previous life. This strongly suggests that maintaining specific bonds is part of the quest undertaken by the soul in terms of reincarnation. We will explore this idea later in the following chapter.

A popular Wiccan teaching found in the text known as the *Charge of the Goddess* addresses a type of quest. The teaching states "*If that which you seek is not found within you, you shall never find it from without.*" In essence, this means if what we seek is not already within us then we will never realize it through any outward worldly experiences. But if answers reside within us, then where are they and how do we embrace them?

The mystical theme of the sacred or holy quest is found in both pagan and Christian literature. In Christianity, the cauldron becomes a chalice, and like its predecessor it is a vessel that offers regeneration, renewal, and healing. Also, like the cauldron, the chalice gains its power from the liquid it contains. This liquid is a magical or mystical brew waiting within a vessel that is hidden away. It can only be obtained through a purposeful journey.

In keeping with the cauldron theme, the chalice (known as the Holy Grail) is always hidden away in some secret place. In the Grail mythos it is sometimes guarded by specially chosen knights whose pure nature permits them to keep the Grail without misusing its power for selfish gain. In the cauldron mythos, the party that sets out in search of the vessel is always composed of men of great renown. Here we see that this is all about inner natures related to something residing deep within us.

In every tale of the Quest there is danger involved. This danger is always linked to the land in which the vessel is hidden away. In the oldest tales of Quest we find the appearance of a special item that grants safe passage through realms of inherent danger. In northern European tales this is the Silver Bough, a branch taken from a sacred tree with significance to the Faery race. In southern Europe it is a branch known as the Golden Bough. Bearing either branch allows a person to enter and leave the mystical land beyond the mortal world. These lands are called the Faery Realm, the Underworld, or the Otherworld. Like the cauldron and the Grail these places possess magical water (or the water is part of the mystery of the realm).

In some of the oldest myths in Western literature, an interesting theme is found that connects water and memory. One universal idea is that the newly dead arrive with great thirst in the Land of the Dead. As a result they seek to cool their thirst at the springs of the Underworld. In the mystery tradition, we find mention of two springs or wells. One contains the *water of memory* and the other the *water of forgetfulness*. Sometimes they are located at the crossroads in the Underworld where the soul must choose to drink from one or the other.

Greek historian Professor Margaret Alexiou, in her book *The Ritual Lament in Greek Tradition* (1974), writes of souls and the waters of the Underworld. She describes the tears of the living as flowing down into the Underworld to "greet" the dead. These tears are so bountiful that they form a river or lake through which the dead can be reached. Professor Alexiou quotes an unnamed ancient text addressing mourners, that reads:

> *Why do you stand there, orphaned children, like strangers, like passers-by . . .Why do your eyes not run like a quiet river, so that your tears become a lake and make a cool spring, for the unwashed to be washed, for the thirsty ones to drink?*

Alexiou goes on to say that it is this river, lake, or spring that makes contact possible between the living and the dead. Why is this theme of ancestral connection always associated with liquids?

In the context of this book we can once again look at the relevance to DNA in our body fluids. The connection between water and the dead, in the form of tears or blood, is noteworthy (if even as a metaphor). When we look at the quest for the lost cauldron, and the souls seeking to quench their thirst in the Underworld, we see the same powerful drive. It is what motivates the seekers to persevere despite obstacles and setbacks.

Ancient tales depict guardians in the Underworld. Sometimes they stand at the entrance and other times they protect a sacred spring or well. One popular myth tells of a white cypress tree (or poplar tree) beside a spring. The traveler is told to avoid this spring and not to drink its waters. The soul is then instructed to continue on until it comes to the Lake of Memory. Here the soul must introduce itself as a "child of earth and of starry heaven." However, the guardians will not allow the soul to drink unless it confesses to being parched and perishing from lack of water. It must then ask to drink the cool water from the Lake of Memory, at which point the guardians provide some of its water.

In the oldest written tales (those attributed to Homer) we find a tradition of greater antiquity. In one story a group of Greek heroes seek to speak with the dead and so they travel into the Underworld. In order for the dead to reply they must be offered some water mixed with blood in a vessel. Consuming the blood not only allows the dead to speak but we are also told it renders them fully conscious as the people they previously were in life. Here we find that the blood is not only the connection between the living and the dead, it also contains memory.

When we unravel these tales of the Underworld, it becomes clear that at the center they are stories about relationships and communication. If you think about it, the idea of ancestral veneration is a relationship between the living and the dead. We draw something from knowing our heritage, and many of us take pride in our ancestral roots and homeland. But do the dead benefit from our veneration?

One idea is that the dead live on through us, and that part of our work is to see their work completed. Another view is that some of our ancestors are in need of healing due to the type of life they lived. In this view we can help cleanse them by making restitution on their behalf. This is a form of acknowledging and righting past wrongs, which helps release our ancestors from the attachment of the negative energy they drew to themselves in life. Such liberation can allow our ancestors to move back into the cycle of reincarnation. In chapters ten or eleven we will look at ways to assist them.

Working with the Chapter Themes

As we have seen so far in this chapter there is a connection between the living and the dead. In the past our ancestors knew this as well, and they created many myths and legends surrounding this theme. It also permeated their religious beliefs.

Part of the work we can do through the Cauldron of Memory involves patching the gaps of knowledge, and repairing the collapsed bridges of the past that once connected us all. War, politics, and religion have (in many cases) rewritten history and distorted perspectives. It is our task to "re-member" the fragmented past by reintegrating the scattered and scrapped pieces. We must, in effect, perform "reverse engineering" (in a spiritual sense).

The key to this task is discernment through a series of exercises involving three power centers in the mind, body, and spirit. These centers are envisioned as inner cauldrons. The illustration shows the assignment of these centers, which are called the Cauldron of Regeneration, the Cauldron of Abundance, and the Cauldron of Enlightenment.

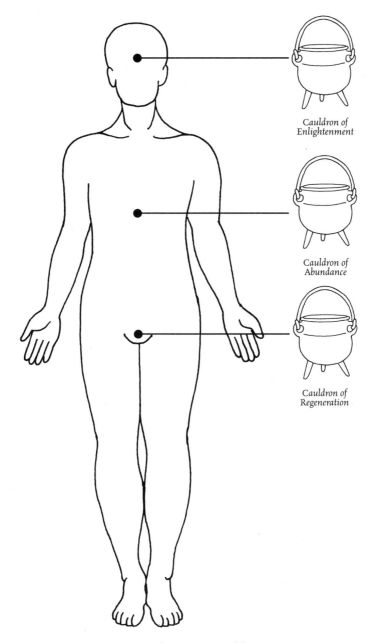

Cauldron of
Enlightenment

Cauldron of
Abundance

Cauldron of
Regeneration

Figure 5: The Inner Cauldrons

As you can see, each cauldron sits at a place of primary function intimately connected to body fluids. In the genital area we find the Cauldron of Regeneration. Here it is linked to our internal reproductive system, which is designed to create new life (generated and sustained by body fluids). In metaphysics, this zone is often referred to as the fire or passion center, and from this area we are vitalized with natural energy.

The next center is the solar plexus, marked by the Cauldron of Abundance. Here it is intimately linked to the heart and to the flow of blood through our circulatory system. In metaphysics this center is commonly known as the heart center, or the center of emotions. The latter gives us a sense of fullness or emptiness in life.

The last center is the head, which is marked by the Cauldron of Enlightenment. Here it is intimately connected to the brain and its cerebrospinal fluid. In metaphysics, the head is the spiritual center where human and divine consciousness can meet and interface. It is from this center that the energy of enlightenment emanates.

Working with the cauldron centers involves the use of cords, which appear in chapter six as the Sacred Tree. This ties in with the concept of the Sacred Bough carried to ensure safe passage. The Sacred Tree tool aids us as a means of descending inward to embrace the cauldron, and then outward to return with the essence of its brew. Practical exercises for this technique follow in this chapter.

There are four pathworks to perform in this chapter. The first one involves contact with the mythical Sacred Bough. This will help align you with the energy of this concept. You will also work with the alignment of initiation, which prepares you to receive deeper levels and to gain broader vision. Next you will create an alignment to "Otherworld" consciousness through the Chthonic Roots pathwork journey. This helps you interface with the energy of traditional altered states of consciousness. All of these journeys are inner planes work.

The final pathwork involves encountering the hidden Cauldron of Memory. Because of all the work that must be done before arriving at this step, you will no doubt feel as labored as one of the quest characters from the ancient myths. This is as it should be because without effort there is no true gain on a metaphysical level.

Before moving on to actually reaching the inner cauldron, we must first understand the use of a vital tool. This item is the Sacred Tree that you constructed in chapter six. You will need to integrate this tool with the pathwork of cauldron retrieval.

Working with the Sacred Tree Cord

There are two primary uses for this tool. The first use is as a shamanic ladder, by which you can access other realms or existence. The second use is to evoke and banish. This is helpful in cleansing ritual space, dealing with undesired spirits, and protecting against psychic or magical attack.

In a previous chapter you were introduced to this tool and instructed to create one. Let us review the symbolism. The top of the Tree is the part with the short ends of the cords. This represents the Three Fates and the Triformis Goddess. The top of the Tree is also the heaven world.

The three center knots symbolize the gates to the three known worlds of our ancestors: Overworld, Middleworld, Underworld. They are used as focal points when meditating and pathworking. The long strands at the bottom of the Tree signify the crossroads leading into the Underworld or Otherworld (respectively the Land of the Dead and the realm of the Elven/Faery).

The Tree is held and manipulated in specific ways. Always begin by placing the center knot in the middle of the palm of your hand. Secure it by folding the index finger and little finger to flank the knot on both sides. This will leave the two center fingers extended outward. The last step is to move the thumb up to touch the part with the three small ends of the cords. We will call this the *Commencement Position*.

Active work with the cord is always initiated by folding the two center fingers over a knot. We will call this the *Activation Position*. The individual realm you are working with is determined by the position of the two center fingers on a specific knot. Therefore, to touch the center knot is to work with the forces of matter. The top knot initiates celestial forces, and the bottom knot rouses chthonic powers. To direct the energy the two center fingers remain enfolding the knot, but the index and little finger

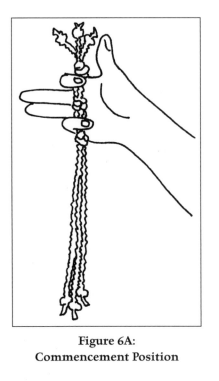

Figure 6A:
Commencement Position

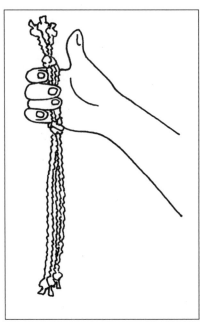

Figure 6B:
Activation Position

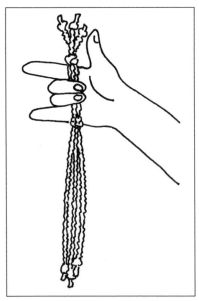

Figure 6C:
Directing Position

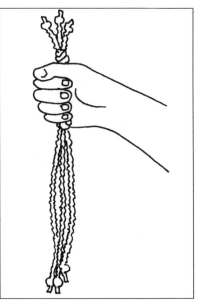

Figure 6D:
Neutralizing Position

are extended and pointing straight out from the palm. We will call this the *Directing Position*.

The Tree hand postures are easy to recall if you remember the order: commence, activate, and direct. To neutralize the Tree, simply fold all your fingers (including your thumb) into the palm area of your hand. Then turn your fist so the palm is oriented upward. Open all your fingers to expose the knots, and with the fingers of the opposite hand grasp the center knot and lift the cord away. We will call this the *Neutralizing Position*. When not in use, put the Tree away in a closed and secure place.

In the following series of pathworkings, you will be holding the Sacred Tree cord in your left hand (left is the receiving side). Before moving on to the next section, spend some time practicing the hand manipulations assigned to the Tree. This will familiarize you with the tool, and handling it will not be awkward and distracting while you are performing the pathworkings. Do not forget to use all the stages of Tree cord work: commence, activate, direct, and neutralize. Always end with neutralizing the Tree.

Pathwork: The Sacred Bough

Study the imagery on this card for a few moments. This is the legendary Sacred Tree that appears in stories about traveling to the Otherworld or Underworld. Suspended on the left is the Silver Bough, a gift from the Faery Queen that allows safe passage to and from her realm. On the right is the Golden Bough, a magical branch that allows safe passage to and from the Underworld. Take note of the terrain in the background.

To begin this pathworking, place your Sacred Tree cord in front of you where it is easily accessible. Now imagine yourself standing at the crossroads. There is a hekataion in its center, and suspended from either side is the sacred bough of myth and legend. It is waiting for you to take it with you on your Quest for the Cauldron of Memory.

You reach out with your left hand and grasp the branch (at this time pick up your Sacred Tree cord and make the activation posture on the middle knot). You now have the Sacred Bough in your hands. Spend a

SACRED BOUGH

moment with this visualization. Feel the object in your hand and affirm to yourself that this guarantees your safe passage.

Imagine yourself walking to the right fork in the crossroads. You choose this path and follow it as it wanders away from the crossroads. The road continues up a steep hill. You make your way up to the top of the hill.

Standing on the hill you are aware of the great height. The wind passes over you and this makes you free—refreshed and alert. You look down at the path descending along the other side of the hill. Below you see the ocean spreading out to the horizon. Spend a few moments with this visualization.

It is time to leave the hilltop. You move down the hillside path. As you walk, the path turns to the left and disappears around a ledge in the distance. You follow the path and discover that you are now walking along the narrow ledge of a cliff high above the ocean. You continue, carefully making your way along the narrow passage.

Ahead of you, you can now see a structure at the end of the cliff. It is the remains of a temple. As you approach, there are seven steps leading up to an altar that is flanked by two temple columns. Each step has a star on the center of it. You walk up the steps to the altar.

The setting looks very familiar. You feel as though you have been here before, but the memory of this place is not of a temple in ruins. You see it pristine and vibrant, and tended by temple maids, priestesses, and priests. As you stand looking at the altar, the wind rushes into the setting and you hear the words "remember me, rebuild me." This makes no real sense in the moment, but you do not dwell on it.

You feel the need to move on, and so you walk down the seven steps, and turning right, you follow the road as it descends toward the ocean. You are walking along the pathway as it widens into a mesa overlooking a wooded area below. The descent into the woods is a gentle slope, and the path appears much wider as it enters the trees. You choose this way and begin walking down to meet the opening in the woods.

Pathwork: Initiation

Study the imagery on this card for a few moments. This is the concept of initiation, a formal joining with established alignments that connects initiates to inner planes forces. Take notice that the initiators wear black robes, the color of procreation and potentiality. In their cupped hands the initiators hold a sphere of energy. This symbolizes the ancient and sacred flame of knowledge and wisdom. In the background is a straight path leading to the horizon where the full moon and stars hover in the night sky. This represents the manifestation of the celestial intelligence, the divine presence of the heaven worlds.

To begin this pathworking, hold your Sacred Tree cord in the activation posture, using the top knot). Imagine you are walking along a road leading into the woods. As you approach the trees, the figure of a woman and a man wearing black robes appear on the path. The man speaks: "*For you to have reached this place, long has been your journey.*" You nod in agreement. The woman speaks: "*What is it you seek on your journey?*"

INITIATION

You look at the woman and then at the man, and reply: "I quest for the Cauldron of Memory." The woman responds "Know that if what you seek is not found within you, you will never recognize it in the outer worlds." The man speaks: "For it has been within you since your beginning, and it waits for you at your journey's end."

The initiators cup their hands together and a sparkling sphere appears. Their voices join as one, as they say: "We are the keepers of the sacred flame of knowledge and wisdom. We pass to you enlightenment in the places of darkness." The couple raises the sphere above your head. It expands, bursts, and then cascades down upon you in a shower of sparkling lights. The tiny sparks begin to swirl for a moment and then form into a spiral around your waist. Then the spiral pours into your body through your navel and disappears from your sight (spend a few moments with this visualization).

The initiators motion for you to follow them, and then turn down a long road flanked on each side by a row of trees. These trees are the lineage bearers, vessels that contain the memory of everything that has transpired throughout time. There is an atmosphere of great reverence in this place and you walk silently with the initiators along the path.

You are walking along the road and you notice a mound of earth in the distance. As you draw near you see an old well set on the mound. This is an ancient place, and you smell the rich earthy fragrance of fertile soil and roots. This is the primal earth known so long ago to your distant ancestors.

Pathwork: Chthonic Roots

Spend a few moments studying the imagery of this card. The well in the picture represents the concept of sacred wells. These are found throughout all Europe and are legendary portals into the hidden realms. Many sacred wells are associated with the pagan cult of the dead, which is rooted in ancestor veneration.

Take note of the plants that are placed on a cloth in front of the well. These are some of the traditional plants used by shamans and witches for trance work and spirit travel. Lying with the roots is a special knife made for harvesting herbs. Here it represents the moon as the harvester of the spiritual essence of these chthonic plants of the Underworld.

To begin this pathworking, hold the Sacred Tree cord using the activation position on the bottom knot. Imagine yourself standing near the sacred well with the initiators beside you. You look down at your feet and notice something bundled in a cloth on the ground. The initiators uncover the bundle to expose several plants. With the plants is a sickle-shaped blade, which begins to glow with a silvery light. Spectral images of humanoid shape rise from the plants and you realize that they are the spirits residing inside the harvested items. Three of them approach you and form a line in front of you from left to right.

The first spirit speaks to you: "*I am the spirit of the hero that is bound to this place. I share power with you.*" The second spirit addresses you: "*I am the healer spirit dwelling above and beneath this place of the holy well. I share power with you.*" The last spirit speaks: "*I am the prophetess who whispers from this place. I share power with you.*"

CHTHONIC ROOTS

The spirits watch you for a response, and you reply "I *am the seeker of the hidden Cauldron of Memory. Will you guide me to what I seek?*" The hero spirit touches your solar plexus, and says: "I *add to your courage*" (spend a moment with this visualization). The healing spirit touches your forehead and says: "I *heal your misconceptions and hardened views that block the way*" (spend a moment with this visualization). The prophetess spirit touches your belly and says: "*The way is clear, the path is inward*" (spend a moment with this visualization).

In front of you is the holy well. You are guided to it by the three spirits. You notice that inside the well a rope ladder is suspended. You climb onto the rim of the well and begin to descend inside the opening. As you climb down there are seven rungs on the ladder (spend a moment with this visualization).

You reach the end of the rope ladder and you are now standing on the top landing of a stone spiral staircase leading further downward (spend a moment with this visualization). You begin to walk down the steps (there are seven). As you descend, you notice that a soft glow of light is coming from your forehead, solar plexus, and belly. This is giving light to the darkness of the staircase (spend a moment with this visualization).

Your seventh step on the stairs brings you to a landing, and you notice another set of seven steps leading off downward to the right. You begin walking down this last set of seven steps. Count them off as you descend: 7-6-5-4-3-2-1. Your last step ends in front of a stone archway that opens into a large cavern (spend a moment with this visualization).

You enter the cavern. It is dimly lit by a fire ring in the distance. You begin to walk slowly toward the fire. As you move along you notice figures of people moving about in the shadows along the edge of the cavern. They wear clothing from all time periods (even back to the era of animal skins). These are all of your ancestors.

You continue to walk toward the fire ring. As you approach, you see a cauldron set over the fire, and around this are nine maidens in white hooded robes. They appear to be tending the cauldron. You stand now in front of the maidens and they all turn to look at you. These are the Muses of myth and legend.

Pathwork: The Lost Cauldron

Spend a few moments studying the imagery of this card. This image represents the inner cauldron at the center of your being. Rising up from the cauldron a spiral appears in the steam. This is a symbol of transformation, a sign at the gateway of death and the return to new life. The brew within the cauldron is the "soup" of your own material makeup, as well as the condensed genetic memory of your lineage. But it also contains the memory of all who have lived upon the earth.

Begin this pathworking by holding the Sacred Tree cord in the activation position, using the bottom knot. Pause for a moment, and then with the fingers of your right hand, grasp hold of the three small ends of the cord on top of the Tree. Then slide your left hand down the long strands until you reach the end knots (stop there).

Visualize the cauldron in front of you. Its steam rises up and forms the double helix shape. In the center a spiral emerges and then fades

CAULDRON

away, merging back into the steam. It does this three times (spend a few moments with this visualization).

One of the Muses speaks to you, saying, "*Behold the Cauldron of Memory*" and then she dips a ladle into the boiling cauldron. She lifts it back out and then all the Muses blow on the liquid as though to cool it down. After a moment, one of the Muses dips her finger into the ladle. Next, she touches her finger to your lips. You open them and she places a drop on your tongue. She repeats this three times (spend a few moments with this visualization).

After tasting the brew, you are directed by the Muses to sit in front of the cauldron. The Muses join hands around the cauldron and begin to hum an enchantment. As the sound fills the area, the cauldron begins to glow.

You watch the glow as it expands from the cauldron. The glow transforms into a spirit-form replica of the cauldron (spend a few moments with this visualization). The chanting continues and the spirit-form cauldron rises up above the material cauldron. The Muses raise their arms up to meet it.

You observe the spirit-form cauldron floating in the air. The Muses move their arms, directing the floating cauldron and positioning it above your head. Slowly they lower the cauldron of light down on your head. It rests there briefly as the light fills your brain (spend a few moments with this visualization).

The Muses lower the cauldron down until it rests in the area of your solar plexus. The light penetrates into your chest (spend a few moments with this visualization). Finally the Muses lower the cauldron downward and it comes to rest on the ground (encompassing your belly and genital area). In this position the cauldron emanates its last warm sphere of light. The lower half of your body absorbs it, and then the spirit-form cauldron disappears into your body.

The Way of Return

As with the previous pathworking in chapter seven, you must now return to the starting point. Again, we will work in reverse order. By now you should be acclimated to this technique, and therefore I will present a brief journey of return. Remember to take time visualizing each phase as described.

Begin the journey by leaving the physical cauldron and heading back to the archway (hold the ends of the long strands of the Sacred Tree cord in your left hand). Pass through the arch and proceed up the stone staircase. The stairs curve to the left as you ascend. Take seven steps up to the landing.

In front of you is another stairway leading upward. Take seven steps to the landing. Here you see a rope ladder with seven rungs leading up to the opening of the holy well. You climb each rung slowly.

You are now at the rim of the holy well. Climb out and back onto the mound (while visualizing this, grasp the bottom knots with your right hand and then slide your left hand up to the bottom knot above the long strands). Ahead of you is the road you took that led to the holy well. You walk along this path of return. The path continues along and then between a long line of tall trees on both sides of the road. You continue down the trail.

Ahead in the distance, you see the road leading out of the trees. You continue walking. You reach the end of the woods and walk out. In front of you is a road leading up the side of a mesa. You begin climbing up the road. The road takes you to the top of the mesa. In front of you is what remains of an ancient temple. You walk past it and continue homeward.

Continuing on, you see a pathway ahead on the right leading up and along the ledge of a high cliff. You carefully move along this path. The trail continues until the ledge merges with a hillside. You walk up to the top of the hill.

On the other side of the hill you see a hekataion set in the center of a crossroads (slide your left hand up to the center knot). You approach the Tree and return the Sacred Bough, hanging it back on the pole.

Now, slowly take in a deep breath, hold it for a moment, and then slowly release it. Repeat this for a total of three times. Be aware of your physical body, and listen for any and all sounds around you. Finish by having a snack and drink of water or juice.

Working with the Cauldron

The system of inner cauldron work is relatively simple and easy to work with. It relies upon integration and alignment with ancient memory-chains, morphic resonance, and the stepping stone of genetic memory. The pathworkings in this book are essential to establishing this within the individual attempting to make contact with the Cauldron of Memory. If you have not performed each and every pathworking in this chapter and chapters seven and eight, go back and do so now before beginning the following exercises.

The structure of this system includes working with three different inner cauldrons. Each of these is connected with a personal power center of the body, which is aligned with an inner planes counterpart. This is established through the pathworkings. Each of these inner cauldrons can be activated by a simple technique.

Obtain some pennyroyal oil or a plant. The oil or a leaf from the plant is used to anoint each of the three centers. To begin, simply touch the pennyroyal to the area just above the pubic bone. Then do the same at the solar plexus, and end with anointing the forehead. Some people are allergic to pennyroyal; therefore it is wise to test a small amount on your skin before using it. Bear in mind that pennyroyal oil produces a slight tingling or mild burning sensation. This is normal and is not an allergic reaction unless a rash appears. If you are allergic to pennyroyal, try another mint-scented plant or oil.

The primary work with the inner cauldron exercises is designed for retrieving ancestral memory (and other things related to this theme). However, the exercises can also be used as techniques for healing, casting spells, or enhancing personal power. In such cases you can work with one or more of the inner cauldrons, and in whichever order you find suitable. This is covered in chapter thirteen of the book.

The pathworkings you have already performed are now aligned to the Tree cord. The cord has absorbed the resonation of your journey experiences, and it contains the energy imprint and inner planes alignment. This means that you do not have to perform the pathworkings in order to reach the inner Cauldron of Memory.

Inner cauldron work requires a deeper level of Tree cord work. You will descend and ascend the inner levels of your being. This is directed by sliding the cord up or down in accordance with the symbolic knot that corresponds to the specific realm you want to reach. The following exercises will guide you through the necessary steps. For the retrieval of ancestral memory, you will work with all three inner cauldrons in succession.

In this chapter I want you to only read through the cauldron exercises. I do not want you to perform them until you have completed reading the book. There is more for you to know before actually encountering the Cauldron of Memory. However, for now it is important that you read the rest of this chapter thoroughly, as it will acclimate and align you to cauldron work in important and vital ways. In chapter thirteen you will be presented with the practical work to perform as a formal session. At that time we will revisit the following techniques.

Preparation for Cauldron Work

Before working with cauldron retrieval you will need your Stone of Remembrance and the White Serpent cord. Sit comfortably and take these items out of the carrying pouch.

Wrap the white cord loosely around your right wrist and secure it so that it does not unravel. Place the Stone of Remembrance in front of you. Light a candle and some incense for ambiance. You want some lighting, but nothing bright like direct sunshine.

Pick up the Stone of Remembrance and say:

I call upon the memory of all things primal, of fire and earth. I call to the memory sleeping in the sacred land of my ancestors. Awaken, come to me, and guide me to what I seek.

Close the stone in your fist, look at the white cord, and then extend your arm straight out away from your body and say:

White serpent, keeper of the memory of bone, messenger between the realms of the dead and the living, winding current of past, present, and future, awaken and lead me to the hidden memories of my ancestors.

Remain briefly in this position while you visualize the serpent pulling you off to some distant place and time. After a few moments, put the stone down and pick up your Sacred Tree cord in commencement posture. You are ready to move on to the Cauldron of Regeneration work.

EXERCISE SIX: *The Cauldron of Regeneration*

The purpose of this exercise is to use the lower cauldron as a means of regenerating ancestral memory. With this cauldron we boil away the debris, contamination, and the masking that hides the ancient memories from our awareness. In effect, we renew the memories and make them whole once again.

To begin the process, you will assemble the fragments that are associated with what you wish to retrieve. For an example of the basic mechanics, we will focus on the use of a photo of an ancestor that we know little about. Bear in mind that the following is not the actual intended usage of the technique for retrieval in Cauldron of Memory workings. Consider it to be an experiment with the inner process itself.

For our example of how the inner mechanism works, we will use an imaginary photo of a person we will call Aunt Rose. In this scenario you will concentrate on the photo of Aunt Rose and study her in every detail. Take note of anything in the background of the picture. When you are ready to proceed, free your hands and take up your Sacred Tree cord in your left hand.

Position your fingers in the activation posture using the bottom knot. With the fingers of your right hand, hold the three small strands located at the top of the Tree. Now slide your left hand slowly down the long strands until you come to the end knots, and then stop. As you slide your hand, try to feel as though you are descending inward through your body, passing through each center: forehead, solar plexus, and genital area. This feeling of descent is vital, and the more you strengthen it, the more effective retrieval will be. In time you should be able to perform this with great skill, but for now don't get discouraged if things seem hazy. Regard this as a stage of development and continue to work with this technique.

Once your descent is complete, visualize the cauldron in front of you. Mentally transform it into a spirit-form cauldron of energy (identical to the original model). Move this replica into your genital area; visualize the cauldron encompassing the lower half of your body. Spend a few moments with this imagery.

To initiate retrieval, the image of Aunt Rose is mentally lowered into the boiling cauldron. You then think of everything you already know (or think you know) about Rose. Visualize each thing as a drop of liquid and see it fall into the cauldron's brew. Naming each thing is useful as you see it fall into the cauldron (for example, Rose was born in 1895, Rose was a seamstress, etc.). Continue doing this until you have exhausted the known memories.

Begin the next phase by visualizing three drops of blood falling into the cauldron's brew, and then see a spiral form, which then sinks into the cauldron beneath the bubbling surface. After a few moments of meditation, mentally picture the image of Aunt Rose rising from the cauldron. Visualize a sphere of light forming around her until her image is like a figure in a snow globe. Hold this image and then move on to the inner Cauldron of Abundance.

EXERCISE SEVEN: *The Cauldron of Abundance*

In this center of power we begin to join the unknown elements of what we seek with what we already know. In this light, "abundance" is rejoining and revealing what was absent beforehand. To begin, slide your hand from the bottom knot up to the middle knot. Once your hand is on the center knot, activate it.

With your hand in the activation position, visualize the spirit-form cauldron glowing at the center of your solar plexus. The cauldron encompasses the center of your body and fills it with light. Spend a few moments with this imagery. The next step is to visualize the image of Aunt Rose in the snow globe hovering above the cauldron.

With the image of Rose clearly in your inner vision, lower her globe into the cauldron and see it disappear into the brew. Now see in your mind's eye the scattered pieces of a jigsaw puzzle spread out in front of you. These are the missing bits of knowledge that now surround the pieces you already possess (in chapter thirteen we'll address what to do in cases where no previous knowledge exists).

As you look at the fragments of the jigsaw puzzle, visualize a glowing sphere of light drifting down and merging into the scattered pieces. Next, visualize the pieces drawn together into one form as though pulled by a magnet. The jigsaw pieces come together and form the image of Aunt Rose from her picture (but visualize this image much larger than the original picture you had of her).

To complete this exercise, visualize the enlarged image of Aunt Rose rising from the cauldron (still inside the snow globe). Hold this larger image in your mind and then proceed to the next inner cauldron.

EXERCISE EIGHT: *The Cauldron of Enlightenment*

The function of this center of power is discernment. It is here that we integrate into the conscious mind all that is retrieved through the other inner level cauldrons. The Cauldron of Abundance assembled fragmented memories, but the Cauldron of Enlightenment "re-members" the separated components into one cohesive and original whole.

To begin working with this center of power, slide your hand from the center knot up to the top knot, and then activate it. The next step is to visualize the spirit-form cauldron taking shape, and its light completely encompassing your head and neck area. Spend a few moments with this visualization.

With the image of the cauldron firmly in mind, visualize the picture of Aunt Rose rising from the cauldron. Mentally see it suspended over the mouth of the cauldron. Visualize steam rising from the vessel's brew and taking the shape of a double helix (if you have trouble with this image use a simple spiral). Within the steam image see the picture of Aunt Rose turning in the double helix (or in the spiral).

This next step is essential, so put all your effort into it. With the image of Aunt Rose in the helix steam, flare your nostrils out a little, and then inhale through your nose slowly and deeply. Visualize the image being drawn into your nostrils and up into your skull (like the mechanics of a vacuum or a straw). Mentally see the picture of Aunt Rose merging and disappearing into the double helix/spiral. Mentally see the inside of your skull as a hollow space filled with only the steam image of double helix/spiral.

Once you have fully inhaled, lightly exhale while visualizing the helix (or spiral) turning clockwise in your mind. Do not allow your exhalation to make you feel the image is passing out with your breath. Keep the helix/spiral firmly in your mind. Spend a few moments concentrating on the helix/spiral image.

The final phase is to visualize your brain and then see it divided into two halves by the central membrane. Once you have this image clear in your mind, replace the membrane with the double helix image. Complete the

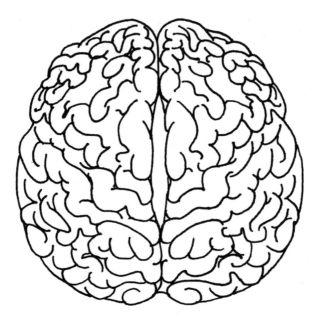

Figure 7: The Left and Right Sides of the Brain with Center Membrane

process by visualizing the double helix generating light so that your brain glows with this energy. Spend a few moments with this visualization.

Take in a deep breath and release it slowly. Allow any and all visualizations to cease. Repeat the deep breathing two more times. Next, slide your left hand down from the top knot to the center, pause for a moment, and then perform the neutralizing posture. Remove the Sacred Tree cord with your right hand and put the cord away for safe keeping. All that remains for full ancestral memory retrieval is to work with the herald's wand.

Using the Herald's Wand

In chapter eight you received instructions on how to create the herald's wand. Its function is to unravel the mysteries and to help you interpret what is revealed. In this section, you are presented with a technique using the wand in conjunction with inner cauldron retrieval.

The herald's wand needs to be prepared for use before performing any cauldron work. To prepare the wand, always wrap the black and red ribbons around it from the top toward the bottom. The pattern resembles candy-cane stripes or the traditional stripes on a barbershop pole. Secure the ends by tying a string or thin cord around them (or, if you must, use a rubber band).

Prior to beginning the cauldron session, place the herald's wand within easy reach. In addition set a pad of paper and a pencil or pen nearby. This will be used for jotting down things while using the wand. Make sure you do not need to get up to reach any of these items. It is important not to disturb the energy for a while following cauldron work.

Begin working with the wand immediately after completing the visualizations. Pick up the wand with your left had and touch the top to each of your body's three power centers: genital, solar plexus, forehead. Then hold the wand upright (vertical) in front of you about chest height. Visualize it glowing with the same light you used in the cauldron session.

Free the ends of the ribbons and visualize the wand transforming into the double helix pattern. Do this for a few moments and then stop. Next, slowly start to unwind the ribbons (going back and forth between the two colors). During this process picture the person, item, or symbol you used in the cauldron. After holding this image for a moment, start to let your mind run a chain of thoughts. Start with the name of the image, speak it out loud, and then say what first comes to mind. Then repeat whatever this is and say the next thing that comes to mind. Do this until both ribbons are completely unwound.

Take up the pad of paper and write down anything that comes to mind, or just start to doodle. Don't try and make sense of anything at this stage. You can write random words, bits and pieces of thoughts, or start to write out a storyline. Let us look at an example. We'll use Aunt Rose again, and let us say all we know about her is that she was our grandmother's cousin. Other than this all we know is what shows in the picture, which is a woman in old-fashioned clothes.

In our spontaneous release of thoughts, we begin by saying "Aunt Rose" and then the next thing that pops up in our mind. This might go something like this: "Aunt Rose ... looks like a nice lady ... lived a long life ... dressed in old-fashioned clothes ... lived far away ... lived in a house on a farm ... had three children ... worked as a seamstress ... broke her leg in a fall … her husband died in the war … she remarried a friend of his … this man worked in a metal shop after the war … this was in New Jersey …" (I wrote this simply allowing my thoughts to run free without an intended direction and without trying to control anything).

Try experimenting with this technique, using someone you know very little about, but can check your impressions with someone else who knows more. Once you have gone through the entire process of cauldron work and the herald wand session, read to this person from your pad and paper. Have them respond with *yes, no,* or I *don't know,* to each thing you bring up. Mark each item so that you can go back and see how accurate your session was (but don't get discouraged if the first several sessions are off track). In time you can improve using this technique. Bear in mind that you are teaching yourself a new form of communication, and you are rewiring the way your mind and body can work together. This usually takes time, although some people do become proficient at it quickly.

One thing to always keep in mind is that people have faulty memories, personal filters that alter perception of events, and they may not know things about a person that were kept secret. Always factor this in when you are looking at the results on your pad and paper. Once you gain confidence with your cauldron work, you can turn to more important matters for retrieval. These are discussed ahead in chapter ten.

The process of using the herald's wand is completed once you have exhausted the free-flowing thoughts you set to paper. When you come to the point that effort is required to think of something, it is time to stop.

Complete your work by touching the herald's wand to your forehead, solar plexus, and genital area. Wrap the ribbons back around the wand and secure the ends. Put the wand away for safe keeping.

Now that you are acclimated by the exercises in this chapter, you are ready to move on to directly contacting your ancestors through the Cauldron of Memory. In a short time you can form powerful bonds and relationships with your ancestors that will benefit both parties. Let us move now to the ancient cauldron and call to those who came before us.

TEN

RETRIEVING ANCESTRAL MEMORY

The Cauldron of Memory is the repository for ancestral knowledge and wisdom. What is lost or hidden from the material realm is secure within the mystical realm of things that cannot be forgotten. The fragile and often political records of what people call *history* pales in comparison to what has actually transpired in the material world. The former does not always match the latter.

The period of pre-history spans a vastly larger period of time than does the era of recorded events. What our ancestors knew and understood in the ages before civilization is only glimpsed today by archaeologists rooting around through bones and ruins. What our ancestors believed and practiced long before the rise of villages and cities is the speculation of anthropologists. The past can seem like a vanishing vapor trail for those who demand that it coincide with the prescribed methodologies of fallible humans.

The ancestral cauldron is the meeting place between the past and the present. It is, metaphorically speaking, the Underworld or Otherworld realm in which the spirits of the dead reside. In this regard we can think of the cauldron as *a state of consciousness*. It is here in the cauldron that the past is as it was, instead of how it is often viewed in modern times.

What was once spoken about at ancient fire pits eventually moved to the hearth side. Here each generation heard the family stories of their ancestors. In the background stood the cauldron, where nourishment

133

simmered in anticipation of the forthcoming meal. Gathering before the hearth and the cauldron was a time for feeding the body and the soul.

When we study the imagery of the ancestral cauldron sitting in the hearth, three elements are symbolic. The fire represents the personal will power of the mind. The cauldron is the material body, and the steam rising from the vessel symbolizes the spirit or indwelling soul. This imagery alerts us to the principle that whatever we *will* through deliberate intention affects the body and spirit.

In this analogy, the body represents the complete internal process of our material makeup. The fire of our *will* can bring forth the mystical vapor of the ancestral memory within our cellular composition. The result is the manifestation of spiritual awareness, which in turn is the materialization of a state of consciousness that is not restricted by the limitations of the human brain. Fortunately we possess a subconscious mind that is not constrained by the conscious mind, which demands a linear analysis.

In the inner mystery tradition, we are taught that humans possess two states of consciousness: the Guardian Mind and the Liberator Mind. The Guardian's primary duty is to secure the well-being of the physical body in accordance with the demands of the material world. The Liberator's responsibility is to ensure that the spirit is not imprisoned by nonmaterial concerns to the degree that it has no relevance to the entire being of the individual.

The Guardian Mind demands that things conform, agree, and operate in prescribed ways. The Liberator Mind inspires the perception that things are not always what they appear to be. The two modes of consciousness were designed to work together in balance, but this union was broken or suppressed long ago by organizations that feared the power of individuals.

Through pathworking with cauldron techniques we can restore the natural inner balance of mind, body, and spirit. At the root of this is the concept that we are spiritual beings temporarily encased in material bodies. Due to this condition, part of our consciousness is required to deal with material existence. This is what we call the "conscious mind" and it is what makes us go to work, eat, sleep, socialize, and so forth.

The term "conscious" is unfortunate in this case because it leads us to believe that our conscious mind is who we are.

The so-called subconscious mind is what reportedly governs our emotional state of being. This, too, is an unfortunate term, because it defines this state of consciousness as secondary in nature. Most modern humans seem unaware that these two halves of our consciousness make up the totality of our consciousness. The two are one and cannot be separated except for discussion and examination. This is evident in the fact that if we deny the needs of one, then we affect the function of the other.

The inner mystery teachings inform us that there are two types of reality in which we realize our participation. One is deemed "material reality" and the other is labeled "nonmaterial reality." Material reality is the perception that we are people living on the earth. The corresponding nonmaterial reality is the perception that we are souls dwelling in physical bodies.

Nonmaterial reality is the perception that we are beings of energy, traveling through inner dimensions in search of expanded enlightenment. The corresponding material reality is that we are mortal beings spending our allotted lifetimes on a planet where we perform tasks in exchange for survival.

Various attempts have been made by humans to reconcile the apparent discrepancy between the material and nonmaterial views of reality. These attempts are known as the construction of various religions and spiritual disciplines. Unfortunately, because most people believe the conscious mind is the real mind, the Guardian Mind causes us to question the reality of opposing religious views. Most people within spiritual disciplines view material reality as an illusion, and so the Liberator Mind causes us to dismiss the idea that wrong and right exist at all.

The intent of cauldron work is to operate under the notion that material reality and nonmaterial reality are two equal halves that when combined in harmony form a third consciousness. This is known as divine consciousness. But what does that mean?

If you look up the word "conscious" in a dictionary, you will find one of its meanings listed as "subjectively known or felt." If you look up "consciousness," one of its definitions is "special awareness" or "alertness to or concern for a particular issue or situation." In this context "divine consciousness" is that which functions without the constraints of our human brain and our spiritual mind. This consciousness is part of us, but we are not it.

Cauldron work, and the associated pathworking journeys, allow us to enter into the realm of divine consciousness without diminishing it due to the addition of our limited human understanding. Instead, we find that our limitations are neutralized in this energy field, and we are directed by a higher stream of consciousness. This form of consciousness can pass unaffected through all realms and is immune to contamination.

When we seek communication and contact with our ancestors, it is vital that we meet them in a realm where we cannot be self-deceived. It is equally important that we do not misguide ourselves through our limited perception of the greater reality that exists outside of us. It is for this reason that we enlist the aid of allies and the god Hermes when doing cauldron work.

Meeting the Ancestors

In this section we will look at the means through which direct contact can be made with the ancestors of our personal lineage. It does not matter if you do not know who they were, or whether you remember them, because they have not lost track of you. Therefore you are not disconnected from your ancestors. At worst, you are not consciously linked. Later in this chapter we will look at the pros and cons of being actively connected.

Meeting the ancestors requires being present in the same realm or state of consciousness. This is where pathworking comes into play. In this section you will find a technique to create a meeting place where you can encounter ancestral consciousness in the form of individual beings. This is facilitated through the aid of Hermes (later you may choose to envision one of your Elven allies).

Another technique involves a form of lucid dreaming. In essence, an idea is planted in your mind as you are falling asleep. The idea surfaces in the dream state and allows you to work with the given theme. The benefit of dream work is that, in dreams, anything is possible. In dreams you can fly, breathe under water, or anything else you need to do in any given situation. We will examine this later in this chapter when we look at the Dream Gate. For now, let us return to meeting the ancestors through the aid of an ally.

The process of meeting the ancestors involves the following preparation and pathworking. Collect the following items:

- Stone of Remembrance
- White Serpent cord
- 1 white candle
- 1 red candle
- 1 black candle
- 1 glass of fresh water
- 1 pin or needle
- Tissue paper

Begin by tying your White Serpent cord around your right wrist. Set the Stone of Remembrance on your work area and place the three candles around it in the pattern of a triangle. The upper tip of the triangle is marked by the red candle. Place it between you and the stone. The other two candles are set behind the stone (white on the left and black on the right).

Prepare a cup or glass of water. Pierce your thumb or finger of the right hand with a pin or needle and squeeze three drops of blood into the water.* Use the tissue paper to help stop the bleeding. Once it stops, light the candles and proceed with the pathworking.

Close your eyes and picture yourself standing at the crossroads with the forks on the road ahead to your left and right. In front of you is the Sacred Tree from which the silver and golden boughs hang suspended. Visualize Hermes walking toward you on the right fork of the road. Spend a moment with this image.

Hermes now stands at your side. He extends his hand and passes his palm across the base of the hekataion. A Faery Door opens just above the

---

* See publisher's note regarding safety on page vi.

base of the trunk. Hermes gestures for you to follow, and you enter the portal.

Inside there is a descending spiral stairway made of old stone. It winds to the right and you follow it downward. There are seven steps; count them as you descend 7-6-5-4-3-2-1. In front of you there is an archway framing a large double door made of wood. The door handles are a pair of goat horns. You pull the horns toward you and the door opens. You step inside.

You are now standing inside a great cavern. There is an opening in the roof overhead. Through this opening the light of the full moon filters downward and sheds a soft light upon the recesses of the cavern. As you look around you realize that this is the same cavern to which you journeyed in search of the cauldron.

In the distance you see the glow of fire in a ring of stones. You walk with Hermes over to the fire, and approaching it you notice the ancient cauldron suspended over the flames. You feel a physical tingling sensation in your body. A soft glow begins to emanate from your forehead, solar plexus, and genital area. These are your three inner cauldrons renewing themselves now in the presence of the ancient Cauldron of Memory.

As you look at the cauldron, the nine Muses appear from the shadows. One of them asks: "*Why have you come to the Cauldron of Memory?*" You reply: "*To meet my ancestor and speak through the river of blood.*" One of the Muses responds: "*Then it shall be as you wish; the way is now open.*"

Hermes gestures for you to wait at the cauldron and then he disappears into the surrounding shadows. You are waiting here with the full moon hovering above you in the opening of the great cavern. Spend a moment with this imagery.

Hermes emerges from the shadows, and with him is one of your ancestors [*spend a moment in discerning the appearance and gender of this ancestor*]. The ancestor raises her or his hands, with their palms displayed. You extend your hands to meet the ancestor's and place your palms on theirs. The ancestor lightly squeezes your hands in the spirit of a warm greeting.

Hermes comes and stands behind you. You feel his hands on your shoulders. He turns you around, facing away from the ancestor. Then Hermes says to you: "*Step back in time*" You take a step backward and your body merges into the ancestor's form. You feel yourself *inside* the ancestor looking out through her or his eyes [*spend a moment with this feeling*].

You are inside the ancestor and the two of you are one being. You find yourself standing in the manner that this ancestor did [*spend a moment in visualization*]. Now you begin to move around the cauldron and find yourself walking as he or she did [*allow the ancestor to pass these sensory feelings of memory to you*].

You are now standing in front of the cauldron. You can sense your ancestor's presence enfolding you, which feels like you are wearing a heavy warm coat [*spend a few moments reflecting on the personality and character of this ancestor*]. You ask the ancestor what her/his name is and you wait for a reply [*spend a moment being receptive to receiving the name*].

Hermes appears in front of you. His hands reach through the merged form of you and your ancestor, and he places them on your shoulders. Hermes says: "*It is time for you to return*" and he pulls you forward and frees you from the body of the ancestor [*spend a moment with this imagery*].

You are now standing facing Hermes. Your ancestor is behind you. You turn to face the ancestor. She or he touches their heart and bows their head in a gesture of respect. You repeat this back to your ancestor. She or he presents you with a small figure of a skull with crossbones. You receive it with your left hand. Hermes then takes the ancestor by the arm and the two disappear back into the shadows.

You turn around, away from the cauldron, and walk back over to the archway where the doors stand open. You pass through the archway, turn and close the double wooden doors. You begin walking back up the stone steps, counting them off: 1-2-3-4-5-6-7.

You are now standing in the hollow of the Sacred Tree. In front of you is the opening that leads back out to the crossroads. You step back through the Faery Door. You turn around to face the Sacred Tree. You bow in respect for what it has offered you through its service as a passageway.

It is time to conclude the pathworking. Pour out the glass of water. Take in three deep breaths, slowly exhaling each time. Become fully aware of the sounds around you, the feeling of your body, and the presence of your surroundings. You are now fully returned to material world reality. Have a snack and a drink of water or juice.

Blow out all the candles, and gather up the items. Return the stone and white cord to your carrying pouch. Clean up any debris and dispose of it by burying it in the earth.

Whenever desired, you can connect with an ancestor through the method you just used. You should meet others over the course of time as well. In the following chapters, you will discover ways of communicating with the ancestors you come to know. These methods involve the use of a cauldron and representations of a skull and crossbones.

Keep a journal to record meeting your ancestors. Write any names you receive, along with general impressions and feelings. Record any messages you obtain, and if possible try to draw a sketch of your ancestor in your journal. You will be connecting back with each ancestor over the course of time.

The Dream Gate

If you have trouble with visualizations, or with pathworking in general, there is another method of ancestor contact at your disposal. This is accomplished through the Dream Gate, which is a portal to a particular area of dream consciousness.

There are essentially two states of consciousness in the dream state. The first level is the one in which the dream dictates a series of events or a storyline. At this level we are subject to the dream and we react to whatever is taking place. In effect we are a drafted actor without a script. In the common dream state our subconscious mind is operational but our conscious mind is a passive spectator.

The second dream level is one where we take conscious control and shape the dream as we wish. This is often referred to as lucid dreaming. The advantage of lucid dreaming (in an occult sense) is that we can come into contact with inner planes realities with both halves of our consciousness fully operational. This allows us to function in the magical setting of the subconscious mind (where anything is possible) while at the same time having the benefits of the conscious mind (where everything has connection and direction).

Lucid dreaming allows us access to what many people call the astral plane. This dimension is one in which thoughts can take on shape. For example a focused thought about wealth can form in an image of cash. The teaching is that the astral dimension consists of a substance that reacts to the energy of anything imprinted on it. By analogy, it is like dipping your finger in melted wax. The wax forms around the finger that entered it, and that portion of the wax takes on the shape of your finger.

When astral substance forms around an impression, we call it a *thought-form* (literally a thought formed into the thing it represents). The teaching is that once something forms in the astral it then sinks into the material realm where it manifests. But we must not mistake daydreams for thought-forms. A daydream lacks the cohesive energy of an intentional thought-form, and therefore the astral substance does not shape around it.

The Dream Gate serves as a means of leaving the common dream state and entering directly into the astral plane. This is accomplished through the visualization of a door in any lucid dream setting. You simply form a door and pass through it into the astral substance. The creation of a lucid state is simple, but requires practice. The simplest method is as follows.

As you are drifting off to sleep, look at your hand. Make the affirmation that while dreaming you will look at your hand. State that when you do, you will become fully conscious in the dream, and you will not wake up in the moment. The latter is important. Repeat this three times as you look at your hand.

With practice you will obtain a lucid state. I suggest that the first time you experience lucid dreaming you simply have fun with it, and shape the dream accordingly. For example, think of someone famous you would like to meet in person. Playing with lucid states will help you learn how things operate.

When you are ready to use the Dream Gate for ancestor contact, you can take advantage of a pre-established image. Begin by studying the illustration of the Moon Tree card. On top of this trellis structure is the

THE MOON

full moon, which rules over the astral plane. In this picture, the moon is flanked by a waxing and waning crescent. These represent the influence of the moon on the astral substance (the ability to form shapes and to dissolve them away).

In the center of the trellis is a crisscross pattern of slats. These represent the connection and intersection of all things. The center pole is the hekataion, which always marks the crossroads (seen or unseen as they may be). Its appearance in the Moon Tree indicates an in-between area, which means that the center of the trellis is a portal between the *rules* of reality. It is the state of realization that exists between the conscious and subconscious mind. To realize something is to make it real.

To implement the Dream Gate, you simply meditate on it before falling asleep. Incorporate this after performing your affirmation of lucid dreaming. This will join your *will* to awaken within the dream to the Dream Gate imagery. Use these three steps before going to sleep:

• Read the pathworking from the previous section.

- Look at your hand and make the affirmation for lucid dreaming.
- Meditate for a couple minutes on the Moon Tree image.

Once you are conscious in the dream, imagine the Moon Tree Gate in front of you. Push on the center pole and the trellis slats will move back, which will create an opening for you to pass through. Slip through this opening and enter the inner planes.

In the background there is a hill. Pass over the hill and visualize a sacred well on the other side. The well has a rope ladder suspended over the opening. The ladder has seven rungs. Climb down the ladder, which will take you into a cavern. In the center of the cavern is a fire pit with the Cauldron of Memory suspended over it. At this point you are at the same place and situation described in the previous section on meeting the ancestors.

The lucid dream technique is not intended to replace the pathworking in the previous section. I have included it for anyone who has trouble with visualization. Using the lucid dream will help enhance your visualization abilities. You will want to perform the actual pathworking process for the full benefits.

Attracting Ancestral Energy

To enhance your connection to ancestral energy, and to more fully activate links, there are several approaches. The basic idea is to immerse yourself in ancestral imagery. This will help awaken cellular memory. In this regard you will be using the magical principle of "like attracts like." Some examples are listening to folk music and traditional music associated with your ancestry, displaying cultural folk art, eating traditional meals, and wearing traditional clothing. These can be combined together or used individually. In either case it should be done as a formal meditation with the intent of making an inner connection.

One way to achieve connection is to choose the cultural item that will serve as your connection and then create the setting. The setting can be music playing in the background while you eat a traditional meal. You might even choose to wear something your ancestors would have worn. When the setting is in place, look at each thing individually.

Pretend that you are one of the ancestors and spend some time in this simple playfulness.

You strengthen connections by spending time in settings that connect to the past. Powerful awakenings can take place by visiting ancient sites of ancestral homelands and places where your ancestors lived and walked about. Seeing this through your own eyes arouses the ancestral spirit within you. Perform this as a conscious and intentional offering to your ancestors. It can elicit profound responses.

Another technique can be used to awaken the ancestral spirit without having to travel to the ancient homeland. This involves seeing precisely what your ancestors frequently saw in their own time period. For this technique we will use the sun, moon, and stars in a conscious and purposeful manner. Let us use the moon as a working model for this process. You can work with the full moon in any month, however October and November are particularly effective times for ancestral work. This is, according to the inner teachings, when the veil separating the worlds is thinnest.

Go out on the night of the full moon between nine p.m. and midnight; if possible choose a rural setting (the less visual presence of modern technology the better). Stand or sit comfortably where you can see the moon without any obstruction. Breathe in and out deeply three times and then say these words as you look at the moon:

This is the very same moon that my ancestors once looked upon. It is not a symbol or representation; it is the one and same moon.

Form a triangle with both your hands by touching the index fingers and thumbs together. This will create a triangular opening. Raise your hands together and position the moon in the center of this opening, and then say these words:

Through you I am joined to my ancestors, who also looked upon you. You are the meeting point. In all time periods, past, present, and future, you are the connection that transcends time.

Figure 8: The Cauldron Posture

Pause for a few moments and then speak the invocation:

Ancestors, the Beloved Ones, I call to you from my time to yours. In the past you once looked upon this moon, as I now look upon it in the present, as my descendant in the future looks upon it. Through this moon we are joined in one time, one space, and one energy.

Bring your hands (still holding the triangular position) to your forehead and press them lightly against your skin. Focus your attention on the moon for a moment, and then close your eyes. Visualize the moon descending as a sphere of light, which enters through the triangle into your head. See it glowing and then move the sphere of light down into your solar plexus and then to your genital area. Visualize a cauldron forming to receive it in each area.

Upon completion of this process, sit comfortably and visualize your entire body as a cauldron. While sitting in the Cauldron Posture, picture yourself as a glowing cauldron of light. Next, focus your attention on your arms, imagining them to be the bowl of the cauldron itself. Once you have this image strongly in your imagination, say these words:

I am open to receiving the ancestral spirit. I welcome my ancestors. I invite my ancestors to communicate with me.

Spend several minutes in a passive state of receptivity. Every time your thoughts stray, repeat the three sentences. Allow your ancestors to speak to you. Do not try and direct this or force anything to happen. Work with this for a while. When you are ready to stop, give thanks to your ancestors (whether you feel you received something or not).

You can perform the stellar connection on any night you choose. However, according to the teachings, the best times for this type of ancestral connection are the months of May and October. During these months the constellation of the Pleiades marks the portals between the worlds. If any of your ancestors were involved in mystical traditions, then this is a good time for you to perform this work. Your attraction to things of a mystical and magical nature is most likely not something new to your bloodline.

Begin by going out at night when the stars are in full view. If possible choose a rural setting where there are as few signs of civilization as possible. Choose a comfortable position from which to gaze at the stars. Breathe in and out deeply three times, and then say these words as you look at the stars:

These are the very same stars that my ancestors once looked upon. They are not a symbol or representation; they are the very same ones.

Form a triangle with both your hands as you did for the lunar exercise. Raise your hands together and position the stars in the center of the triangular opening, and then say these words:

Through you I am joined to my ancestors, who also looked upon you. You are the meeting point. In all time periods, past, present, and future, you are the connection that transcends time.

Pause for a few moments and then speak the invocation:

Ancestors, the Beloved Ones, I call to you from my time to yours. In the past you once looked upon these stars, as I now look upon them in the present, as my descendant in the future now looks upon them. Through these stars we are joined in one time, one space, and one energy.

Bring your hands (still holding the triangular position) to your forehead and press them lightly against your skin. Focus your attention on the stars and then close your eyes. Visualize the stars forming a spiral and then descending as a sphere of light entering through the triangle into your head. Visualize the sphere glowing, and then move it down into your solar plexus, and then to your genital area. Visualize a cauldron forming to receive it in each area.

Upon completion of this process, sit comfortably in the Cauldron Posture. Visualize your entire body as the cauldron itself. While in the Cauldron Posture, visualize yourself glowing as a cauldron of light. Next, focus your attention on your arms, imagining them to form the bowl of the cauldron. Once you have this image strongly in your imagination, say these words:

I am open to receiving the ancestral spirit. I welcome my ancestors. I invite my ancestors to communicate with me.

Spend several minutes in a passive state of receptivity. Every time your thoughts stray, repeat the three sentences. Allow your ancestors to speak to you. Do not try and direct this or force anything to happen. Work with this for a while. When you are ready to stop, give thanks to your ancestors (whether you feel you received something or not).

Now let us look at a solar connection. Choose the traditional day of an ancient festival that held meaning for your ancestors. Research several options and choose one that calls to you. Some examples of celebrations your ancestors surely participated in are planting and harvesting times, which typically fell on or around an equinox or solstice.

Go out just after sunrise or at noon on the day of an equinox and again on a solstice day; if possible choose a rural setting. Stand or sit comfortably where you can see the sun without any obstruction. Breathe in and out deeply three times, and then say these words as you look at the sun:

This is the very same sun that my ancestors once looked upon. It is not a symbol or representation; it is the one and same sun.

Form a triangle with both your hands by touching the index fingers and thumbs together (thereby creating a triangular opening). Raise your hands together and position the sun in the center of this opening, and then say these words:

Through you I am joined to my ancestors who also looked upon you. You are the meeting point. In all time periods, past, present, and future, you are the connection that transcends time.

Pause for a few moments and then speak the invocation:

Ancestors, the Beloved Ones, I call to you from my time to yours. In the past you looked upon this sun, as I now look upon it in the present, as my descendant in the future looks upon it. Through this sun we are joined in one time, one space, and one energy.

Bring your hands (still holding the triangular position) to your forehead and press them lightly against your skin. Focus your attention on the sun and then close your eyes. Visualize the sun descending as a sphere of light, which enters through the triangle into your head. See it glowing and then move the sphere of light down into your solar plexus and then to your genital area. Visualize a cauldron forming to receive it in each area.

Upon completion of this process, sit comfortably and visualize your entire body as a cauldron. While sitting in the Cauldron Posture, imagine yourself glowing as a cauldron of light. Next, focus your attention on your arms, imagining they form the bowl of the cauldron. Once you have this image strongly in your imagination, say these words:

I am open to receiving the ancestral spirit. I welcome my ancestors. I invite my ancestors to communicate with me.

Spend several minutes in a passive state of receptivity. Every time your thoughts stray, repeat the three sentences. Allow your ancestors to speak to you. Do not try and direct this or force anything to happen. Work with this for a while. When you are ready to stop, give thanks to your ancestors (whether you feel you received something or not).

Becoming the Cauldron of Memory

In this section we will undertake the process of receiving information from our ancestors and from the memories that flow through time on the wave of morphic resonance. To fully understand how to reconstruct the past through cauldron retrieval, you will need to finish reading this book and working with the techniques. The more experienced you become, the more effective retrieval will become.

Always prepare for retrieval by first making direct contact with your ancestors through one or more techniques provided in this book. When working with ancestors, you will only be able to retrieve the things they have knowledge about. If you wish to retrieve information about other things, then you will need to call upon your allies and/or make connection with morphic energies. We will look at each method in this chapter. Let us begin with the ancestral current.

Method 1: Receiving the Ancestral Current
Required items:

- Sacred Tree Cord
- Stone of Remembrance
- White Serpent cord
- Image related to the information you seek
- A chalice or cup filled with fresh water
- Skull representation
- Red candle
- A bottle of blue food coloring
- A thimble
- Paper and pencil for notes

For the purposes of reference, we will call the following technique "the Cauldron of Reception." The most effective means of achieving retrieval results is to use a representative photo or drawing as a focal point of what you seek. For example, if you want to tap into inner knowledge about Stonehenge then you will set an image of the site in front of you. To actually be present at an ancient site is ideal for retrieval work, or to hold something of antiquity in your hand is likewise beneficial.

Prepare your work area by setting the cauldron as your centerpiece. In front of the cauldron goes the skull, and the red candle is adhered to the top. Wrap the White Serpent cord around your right wrist.

Set the glass of water on the left side of the skull along with the thimble. Squeeze three drops of blue food coloring into the thimble. Light the candle and hold the Stone of Remembrance in your left hand. Finally, set the focal point image directly in front of you, and place the Sacred Tree cord in your right hand.

Begin by sitting comfortably in the Cauldron Posture. Look at the focal item and spend a few moments thinking about what is known about it. When you have exhausted your own knowledge, then look intently at the item and visualize it glowing with blue light. Next, visualize a sphere of blue light rising from the focal item. Give the sphere a name that signifies it (speak this out loud). Focus your mind on the blue sphere of light, form the commencement position on the Tree cords, and say the following words:

I send you to my ancestors to join with the memory of your own time.

Now, visualize the full moon hovering above the western horizon just before moonset. Say the name you gave to the blue sphere, and then picture the full moon transforming into the sphere itself. Say these words:

Descend now into the realm of the ancestral spirit. Take with you my request for further knowledge [perform the activation position on the large bottom knot].

Visualize the blue sphere descending and disappearing beneath the horizon. Spend a few moments with this imagery. When you are ready to proceed visualize the setting of the Great Cavern where the Cauldron of Memory hangs suspended over a fire. Visualize the sphere of blue light manifesting above the cauldron. Begin the following pathwork.

You can see figures moving from the shadows. They approach the blue sphere. These are some of your ancestors and they are called to the blue light because they possess memory about what it represents. Your ancestors join hands in a circle around the cauldron. They look up at the blue sphere. In response the sphere becomes a mist. The mist drifts down and is breathed in by your ancestors. You watch your ancestors for a few moments. They smile with the reminiscence of these memories.

You see your ancestors taking in a deep breath, and together they exhale the blue mist out over the Cauldron of Memory. The mist swirls and descends into the cauldron's brew. Here the memories merge from pieces into a whole.

You now see the blue sphere rising from the Cauldron of Memory. It carries with it the answers to your questions, as known by those who came before you. Your ancestors raise their arms upward and the blue sphere is uplifted from the cavern. It is returning back to you [end formal pathworking, and activate the large center knot on the Tree cords].

Visualize the blue sphere hovering in front of you and above the glass of water. Neutralize the Sacred Tree cord, set it down and pick up the thimble with your right hand and hold it in front of you. Visualize the sphere of blue descending into the thimble and disappear. Then, pour the contents of the thimble into the glass of water. Watch the blue color move through the water. Pick up the glass and say:

> *Here are the ancestral memories returned to me from the past. I receive them and bring them to full consciousness within my entire being.*

Complete the process by immediately drinking the water. Next, sit or lie down and allow time for reflection and meditation. Keep the Stone of Remembrance and the Serpent cord with you. Have the paper and pencil within reach so that you can jot down thoughts that come to you.

When you are finished, clean up the debris and return all the items back to their original location.

Method 2: Receiving Morphic Resonance
Required items:

- Sacred Tree cord
- Stone of Remembrance
- White Serpent cord
- Image related to the information you seek
- A chalice or cup filled with fresh water
- Skull representation
- Red candle
- A bottle of blue food coloring
- A thimble
- Paper and pencil for notes

In this section we will look at tapping into ancient memories that are not directly associated with bloodline lineage. As with the previous exercise, the most effective means of achieving retrieval results is the use of a focal point.

Prepare your work area by setting the cauldron as your centerpiece. Place the skull in front of the cauldron, with a red candle adhered to the top. Wrap the Serpent cord around your right wrist. Set the glass of water on the left side of the skull, along with the thimble. Squeeze three drops of blue food coloring into the thimble. Place the focal point image directly in front of you. Finally, light the candle and hold the Stone of Remembrance in your left hand. Place the Sacred Tree cord in your right hand.

Begin the retrieval process by sitting comfortably in the cauldron position. Look at the focal item and spend a few moments recalling what is known about it. When finished, look intently at the item and visualize it glowing with blue light. Next, visualize a sphere of blue light rising from the focal item. Give the sphere a name that signifies it (speak this out loud). Focus your mind on the blue sphere of light, form the commencement position on the Tree cords, and say the following words:

I *send you into the ancient memory of the earth. I send you to join with the voices of oak and boulder spoken in your own time.*

Now, visualize the full moon hovering above a gigantic tree. Say the name you gave to the blue sphere, and then picture the full moon transforming into the sphere itself. Say these words:

Descend now into the sacred land. Take with you my request for further knowledge [perform the activation position on the bottom knot].

Visualize the blue sphere descending into the tree branches where it becomes absorbed. Visualize the branches glowing with blue light. Now mentally move the light down into the trunk of the tree and visualize the blue glow. Finally, picture the light moving down into the roots. Slide your fingers to the ends of the long cords. Visualize the roots glowing with blue light. Spend a few moments with this imagery.

When you are ready to proceed, visualize the setting of the Great Cavern where the Cauldron of Memory hangs suspended over a fire. Visualize the sphere of blue light manifesting above the cauldron. Begin the following pathwork.

You can see Muses at the Cauldron of Memory as they look upon the blue sphere. They join hands in a circle around the cauldron, and in response the sphere becomes a mist. The mist drifts down and is breathed in by the Muses. You watch them for a few moments as they smile over their old memories.

You see the Muses take a deep breath in, and together they exhale the blue mist out over the Cauldron of Memory. The mist swirls and descends into the cauldron's brew. Here the memories merge from pieces into a whole.

You now see the blue sphere rising from the Cauldron of Memory. It carries with it the answers to your questions as remembered by the spirit of the land. The Muses raise their arms, and the blue sphere is lifted up from the cavern. It is returning back to you [end formal pathworking and slide your fingers back up to the large bottom knot, and then activate the large center knot on your Sacred Tree cord].

Visualize the blue sphere hovering in front of you and above the glass of water. Put the Sacred Tree cord down, pick up the thimble with your right hand and hold it in front of you. Visualize the sphere of blue descending into the thimble and disappear. Then, pour the contents of the thimble into the glass of water. Watch the blue color move through the water. Pick up the glass and say:

Here are the memories from the sacred land returned to me from the past. I receive them and bring them to full consciousness within my entire being.

Neutralize the Sacred Tree cord. Complete the above process by immediately drinking the water. Next, sit or lie down and allow time for reflection and meditation. Keep the Stone of Remembrance and the Serpent cord with you. Have the paper and pencil within reach so that you can jot down thoughts that come to you. When you are finished, clean up the debris and return all the items to their original location.

The two preceding exercises provide a good working formula for retrieval work. If you desire you can modify them or create ones that work better for you. Keep in mind, however, that these models are constructed on functioning foundations that adhere to time-proven occult techniques. Therefore I encourage you to try to keep the basic mechanics in place.

The sections in this chapter have introduced you to ancestral contact and alignments. In the next chapter we will explore ways in which this can be applied to daily life and the spiritual path that gives meaning to life. Let us continue onward.

ELEVEN

THE SKULL AND CROSSBONES

In this chapter we will explore specific elements related to ancestral wisdom and its communication. We will also examine techniques associated with these themes. The foundation of the concepts in this chapter is built upon the belief that death does not extinguish consciousness. This is, of course, an ancient belief and one shared in modern times as well. It is also the basis for religious belief.

Over the course of time there have been many different views concerning life after death. These views vary from the idea of the dead being bound to the grave site, to the notion that the dead move on to another world outside of the mortal realm. Mixed with this idea we find the belief in an awaiting reward or punishment. Among the diverse concepts we must also include reincarnation.

One lesser-known idea regarding the dead is that they dwell within us in some inner-dimensional way. This relates to one view held by the ancient Celts. They collected severed heads and kept the skulls in the belief that this captured the knowledge, wisdom, and experience of the original owners. This joins an ancient belief that within the skull is retained the consciousness of the person who animated it in life. Therefore to possess skulls was to hold access to the experience of many lifetimes.

The skull, as a mystical figure, shows up in many sources. Its most classic appearance is when coupled with a set of crossbones. This imagery, in effect, fixes the skull in place and represents the presence of the ancestral memory. In some ritual and magical images, the skull is paired with a cauldron—another mystical symbol. Additionally, we often see the occult presentation of the skull sitting on a fireplace mantel with a stack of books. This is powerful imagery in connection with ancestral knowledge.

When we think of the ancestral hearth, we often picture the family cauldron suspended over the fire. Old fireplaces were very large compared to contemporary ones—the openings on some large enough for a person to easily step inside the hearth space. We will see the importance of this later on in this chapter and the next one.

Drawings and paintings of mystical cauldrons at the hearth frequently include images of a human skull with crossbones in front of it. This is very common in Halloween images as well as depictions of the witches' Sabbat. In most cases the artist meant only to demonstrate something macabre and was perhaps not aware of the underlying mystical associations.

In occult tradition, the skull is used to represent ancestral wisdom and knowledge, as well as secret teachings and mysteries. In esoteric systems, the crossbones often symbolize gates. The crossed bones indicate something that is hidden, locked, or protected. This is the occult meaning behind why crossbones are set in front of the skull.

The skull and crossbones appear very often in front of a cauldron. In such cases the cauldron can be viewed as a symbol of regeneration and as the Mother Goddess, who is a deity that generates life and then receives it back again at death. As a composite image the skull, crossbones, and hearth make a statement: *Hidden here is the ancient knowledge that leads to immortality.*

In ancient times it was believed that to be remembered was to achieve immortality. This was often the ultimate goal of heroic deeds and heroic lives. To have one's name live on in legend was to achieve everlasting life. To be forgotten in time was to perish forever.

One of the gifts of the Cauldron of Memory is that it ensures no one is ever truly forgotten. All of our ancestors live on through the river of blood that flows from generation to generation. One of the ways in which we can honor our ancestors is to become a Cauldron Keeper. This role is presented in the last chapter of this book.

Communication with ancestral spirits is key to working with them and experiencing the benefits. Over the course of time, various inner traditions have grown around this subject matter. Some common and well-known methods include holding a séance or using a Ouija board. A lesser-known method is to use the skull and crossbones. To effectively use this method requires that the practitioner keep an ancestral shrine where he or she actively performs ancestral veneration.

Ancestral Veneration

In modern society there is a tendency to separate the dead from the living by establishing cemeteries in areas often far away from housing areas. Individuals tend to die in hospitals and the system carries them away and deals with them sight unseen. In ancient times people often died in their own family homes and the body was prepared for burial or cremation by the family. The dead were remembered at various times of the year, just as today we celebrate the birthdays of friends and loved ones.

Remembering and honoring your ancestors directly connects you to your roots. In this fast-paced and ever-changing world, this one celebratory act is intimately yours and belongs to you as an individual. Through it you can draw power and vitality, for it is in experiencing the momentum of the past that you can truly realize who you are today. Understanding who you are today prepares you to reap the harvest of what you can become tomorrow.

Looking back at the past, we find that the ancient Etruscans worshipped their ancestors as Lasa spirits. These spirits were known to the ancient Cult of the Dead, and later merged with the belief in a Faery race. The Lasa were associated with fields, burrows, and mounds. This association is also attached to Faeries in common lore, myth, and legend.

The ancient Romans called such spirits Lare and Penates, and saw them as household spirits, guardians of home and family. Small shrines were set by the hearth or upon the mantle in remembrance of departed loved ones. Candles were lighted when a family member was born, wed, gave birth, or died. In this way the ancestral spirits participated in the family event, and the momentum of the ancestral current was kept flowing within the family. Offerings were also placed at the shrine when a new venture was undertaken or a dilemma faced the household. This was performed in a belief that family spirits in the Other World had power to influence the world of the living.

In modern times, we can connect with the ancestral spirit in much the same way as did our distant relatives. A personal alignment can be established by something as simple as lighting a candle at your ancestral shrine and reading the myths or legends associated with your heritage out loud. In this case the spoken voice creates vibrations carrying the passion of your blood up into the ether. This creates a ripple within the astral plane, connecting you with times and people long forgotten.

To strengthen this connection you can place symbols or icons typically associated with your nationality in or around the shrine. It is also useful to take on a personal name that may have been used in ancient times among your ancestors. This helps to further connect you with the energies of antiquity. Reading books and viewing movies that reflect cultural heroes is also an excellent aid to personal alignment because it stirs the blood. These tales often transmit the link to the collective conscious and subconscious of the ancient peoples who created them. Therefore, by incorporating them into your own consciousness you become a living part of the spiritual heritage of your ancestors.

Preparation of an Ancestral Shrine

Maintaining an ancestral shrine helps to encourage the flow of energy from the ancestral spirit. Therefore you will find it beneficial to create one in your home or on your property. Select a suitable form of shrine structure that reflects the culture of your ancestry. For example, select a Greek or Roman temple façade if you are of southern European lineage, or a rustic stone or wooden one to suit northern European antiquity. In effect, this will be the home of your family spirit, so make it attractive and inviting.

Ideally you will want to suspend the shrine on a wall, or place it on a mantel. Try to align the shrine with an orientation to the west or east; this will symbolically connect it to the rising and setting of the sun and moon. In this way you create a connection to the cycles of life, death, and rebirth. Set a small figurine in the shrine to represent the indwelling spirit. If possible its physical appearance should reflect your nationality (and you can place more than one figure on your shrine). You can also set pictures of departed family members on your shrine.

Your shrine will serve as a type of altar space upon which you can make offerings to your ancestors. Typically you will place a small offering bowl or vase in front of the shrine. Offerings of grain, milk, or flowers are good choices. To activate the shrine, you can light some incense that you find appropriate and meaningful. Pass the smoke beneath the shrine so that it rises up and around the shrine. While doing this, say:

Spirits of the air, awaken, gather the ancient ones here, who were of old known to my Clan. I bless this shrine in the names of [give your deity names]. As it was in the time of the beginning, so is it now, so shall it be.

Now, sit quietly before the shrine and visualize a small soft blue light around the figurine or statue in your shrine. In time you can actually see this light come and go within the shrine, assuming that you provide an offering at each full moon and all family occasions such as birthdays, marriages, and so forth.

To keep a connection to your shrine, and personal rapport with your ancestors, light a candle on your shrine every day. Spend a few moments in reverence each time you sit before the shrine. Ask for assistance and guidance in personal matters, and work toward establishing a good rapport with your ancestral spirit. You can and should combine cauldron work with your session before the ancestral shrine.

When working with your shrine, always keep it clean. Remove the offerings each day. Never leave them longer than twenty-four hours. This is particularly important when offering something that will show obvious signs of decay. Bear in mind that what sits on or in front of your shrine is what you are offering to your ancestors. If this becomes rotten fruit, moldy cheese, or soured milk, then this is what you have, in effect, given to your ancestral spirit. Please do not learn the folly of this through personal experience.

Using the Skull and Crossbones

Once you feel comfortable that a healthy rapport with your ancestors has been established, you can proceed to the next step. This phase involves working directly with the skull and crossbones. You will need to set these items on a separate space other than your shrine. We will refer to this as your altar.

Place the skull directly in the center of your altar space. Fix a red candle on to the top of the skull. In front of the skull, place a small bowl of fresh water. Next, set the crossbones in an X pattern in front of the bowl. Take your White Serpent cord and wrap it around the base of the candle. With this initial setup you are ready to begin.

Light the red candle and say: "I *stir the river of blood with the ripple of life.*" Then, prick your finger and place three drops of blood in the water. Use something to stop the blood flow on your finger. Once your finger has stopped actively producing blood you can move on to the next step.

Separate the crossbones and place them lengthwise and parallel to one another. This forms a pathway leading to the skull in front of you. As you separate the crossbones say these words:

I *open the gates between the mortal realm and the dwelling place of my ancestors.*

Next, reach through the opened way, and remove the White Serpent cord from the candle. Place it in your left hand and move it back to you, passing in-between the bones. Once the cord has cleared the bones, wrap it comfortably around your left wrist and secure it. As you do, say these words:

Figure 9A: Ancestral Portal in Closed Position

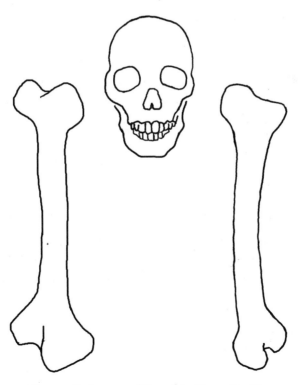

Figure 9B: Ancestral Portal in Open Position

White Serpent, messenger between the worlds, carry to me the voices of my ancestors who dwell beyond the veil. Join us together: past and present [visualize a living serpent coiling around your wrist].

With the serpent cord in place, look into the eyes of the skull. Spend a few moments connecting with the image of the skull as the past. The old saying that the "eyes are the windows of the soul" applies here. You are looking through the skull and seeing your ancestral spirit. It is looking back at you and seeing its current manifestation in your physical form.

During this phase you can speak to and with your ancestors. This is also a good opportunity to make peace where unrest is at play. To forgive and to be forgiven is a spiritual practice. You can also offer prayers to your ancestors and on their behalf. When my father died several years ago, I said to the "powers that be" that I do not hold this soul accountable for any injury or offense done to me, intentional or otherwise. I added that therefore this soul owes nothing in the Otherworld by way of restitution. This is one way of offering liberation to the departed and to yourself.

While working with the ancestral spirit, keep a pen and paper handy to jot down thoughts and feelings. These are valuable to reflect back upon at a later time. If something feels unclear or seems unanswered, ask to be answered in a dream. Sometimes this is the most effective way for communicating because the conscious mind is not in the way. When working with ancestral spirits you will find that they enter your dreams whether or not you have made the request. It is simply the way of things.

At a time of your choosing, you can begin to end the session with your ancestral spirit. This is accomplished through a few simple steps. Begin by formally releasing the ancestral spirit with these words:

Spirits of my ancestors, I thank you for coming into communication with me. I bid you depart now in peace and return to the realm where you dwell. May there always be peace between us.

Remove the bowl of water with your blood in it, and unwrap the Serpent cord. Place it back around the base of the red candle. Next, close the crossbones by laying them in the X pattern. All that remains now is to blow out the candle flame. End with this affirmation:

The ancestral spirits are now departed from the world of mortal kind. They dwell now at home in the land beyond. The gates between the living and the dead are closed once again.

To neutralize this spirit work, pour out the bowl of liquid on the earth (do not pour it down a sink or flush it in the toilet). Remove all the items on your altar work space. Clean the wax up, removing all traces of it, and bury the wax in the earth or boil it away in a pan. If performing the latter, make sure there is an open window nearby. In this way the energy can leave the home and not form a residual layer of energy.

If you want to add more protection, you can evoke Hermes to protect and aid you prior to performing skull and crossbones work. You can also request that he escort the ancestral spirits back to their own realm or inner dimension. This is useful in assuring that nothing undesired remains behind. There is a reason why the Universe maintains a separation of the dead from the living.

Now that we have explored working with ancestral spirits, it will deepen our understanding and practice because we comprehend the inner spiritual traditions and customs associated with the settings for ancestral communication. This is what the next chapter offers, and so let us turn the page and look into the heart and soul of ancient tradition.

TWELVE

SACRED FIRE, HEARTH, AND CAULDRON

In this chapter we will focus on the mystical theme of the sacred fire and on the concept of the hearth as the temple of the flame. Fire is one of the most ancient representations of the divine, and was originally perceived as a feminine force. It is from this archaic concept that the goddess Hestia or Vesta originated. This divine fire theme appears in many cultures where we find goddesses of fire such as Brigit, Pele, and Chantico.

For primitive people, fire required considerable effort to produce and was therefore kept alive by tending to it throughout the day and night. Fire was not only important for daily needs, but was also desired in religious ceremony. The hearth, as the fire place, became the center of family life. This was later expanded into larger political units: the tribe, the city, and the state.

In ancient Greece each city had a common hearth in its civic center. Various ancient writings refer to the legendary structure in Athens known as the Prytaneion. This building was a civic center that featured a common hearth, which represented the collective life and soul of the community. Greek colonists were known to "transfer sacred fire" by taking it with them from their mother-cities. It was drawn from the perpetual fire of Hestia that burned in the common hearth. Transmission from one settlement to another represented a continuing and unbroken bond.

Architectural historian William Lethaby, in his book *Architecture, Mysticism and Myth* (2007), notes that the hearth was specially identified with the omphalos stone, and that the stone was the altar of the sacred fire of Hestia. Lethaby refers to the hearth as the center of the world (which is also the description of the omphalos stone) and depicts it as the "navel of the earth" because it was in the midst of family life.

In northern Europe we find that villages possessed a central fire from which hearths could be re-lighted, and the theme of sacred fire is reflected in the bonfires of such festivals as Beltane. This may be a surviving element of the old hearth cult in which we find the tradition of keeping a perpetual fire. One example is the ancient *need fire*, a custom that involved extinguishing all hearth fires and re-lighting them from a specially prepared fire. The purpose of this fire was, in times of strife, to renew the spirit of the land and therefore the kingdom itself.

The earliest historical references to Beltane fires appear in the writings of Julius Caesar, composed during his military campaign against the Celts. The Beltane tradition of lighting bonfires involved a specific ritual. This required the selection of a hill overlooking the village. Men prepared the setting by first cutting the turf away in a circle or square. A block of turf was placed in the center and firewood was laid in a cross-hatched pattern. The woodpile was then decorated with wool ribbons and flowers (hawthorn when the season allowed).

When a pre-arranged signal was given from the hilltop, all the hearth fires of the village were then extinguished. Afterward, the people gathered at the hill, carrying with them the ingredients for a communal feast. Once the ritual festivities ended, the ashes from the Beltane fires were spread from field to field in a belief that they made the land fertile.

The need fire ceremony, like the Greek custom associated with the Prytaneion, is a ritual of transmission. Once the sacred fire was lighted, runners carrying torches went from home to home re-lighting the hearth fires. In this way the renewed spirit of the land was passed into each home. Thereafter each hearth burned with the revitalized spirit.

Hearth customs were very important to our ancestors. These included traditions centered on marriage, birth, and death. Many of the associated traditions reflect primitive pagan beliefs. These are traceable to ancestral veneration of household and family guardians such as the Penates and the Lare. This practice is reflective of an even earlier custom focused on the household spirit as a Faery.

The concept of the hearth as the residence of a house spirit is illustrated by many fragments of Faery mythology. One belief held that Faery women danced and reveled before the hearth in ways that were inappropriate at proper Faery court. This seems to mark a period of transition at which time some Faeries were yet to be regarded as a higher order of spirits.

In Ireland the Faeries were believed to visit the farmhouses in their district on particular nights. In anticipation the family collected the embers, swept the hearth, and set a vessel of water out for Faery use. In return the family believed that the Faerie would bestow blessings and good fortune. This basic theme is indicative of a time when fanciful folk tales tell of household Faeries doing all the chores while the family is asleep.

The association of Faeries with the hearth may be one of the reasons it was perceived as magical, based on the belief that the hearth possessed a protective nature. For example, an old Cornwall folk magic tradition held that whenever some mysterious ill fate befell a family, a member was required to touch the cravel (the mantle-stone across the head of the open fireplace chimney) with his or her forehead. Afterward, a handful of dry grass was tossed into the fire. The practice of touching the cravel was regarded as the most effective means of averting evil forces.

There is a great deal of confusion between Faeries and ancestral guardian spirits as they connect with hearth customs and traditions. The further back in time we look, the more the distinctions blur together. The earliest pieces of lore indicate a belief that Faeries and spirits of the dead are the same entities. This is noted in material about ancient burial mounds that were also known as Faery mounds.

The lore of mounds, Faeries, ancestors, and the hearth culminates in one folkloric character in particular who is known as Befana. This figure appears in Italian folklore tradition as a Faery, a witch, and a gift-giver (all depicted as an old crone). In this tradition Befana is said to enter the home through the chimney. Once inside she fills stockings and leaves presents in the manner of Santa Claus.

Italian anthropologists Claudia and Luigi Manciocco, in their book *Una Casa Senza Porte* (*The House Without a Door*, 1995), trace Befana back to her Neolithic origins as a fertility goddess. This is later reflected in nineteenth-century engravings that depict Befana sitting in the midst of an abundant harvest, and others showing her dispensing food to a crowd in the public square.

The team of anthropologists describes the ancient Neolithic huts of our ancestors. These dwellings had no door and the only way in or out was through a single hole in the roof. This hole also allowed smoke from the fire pit to rise up and exit the house. It is here that we find the roots of the belief that spirits of the dead could enter and exit their burial mounds, which also featured a hole. Some anthropologists believe that the burial mound was later transformed into the Faery mound of myth and legend.

Claudia and Luigi Manciocco present evidence that Befana is the mediator between the past generation and the current one. As such she joins together the spirits of dead ancestors with the living generation. Through this connection the family lineage is preserved and carried into the future through the children.

In the customs associated with Befana we find the sacred fire. This tradition involves constructing a wooden effigy of Befana depicting her holding a spindle and distaff. The effigy is stuffed with grapes, dried figs, chestnuts, pears, apples, carobs, sweets, and liquor-filled candy. Later it is sawed open and the items are dispensed to the town folk, followed by the burning of Befana upon a pyre.

To burn Befana, a large conical pyre is constructed consisting of several layers made of chopped wood, brambles, horse chestnuts, and straw. The burning of Befana is intended to return life back to the earth, so she is set on fire and burned until only ashes remain. These ashes are then scattered in the fields that will be used in spring planting.

In this custom, we see the theme of the old life of winter decay feeding the new life issuing forth in spring. The crone image of Befana is merely the reflection of her having aged by winter. On the Spring Equinox, Befana is born again, life is renewed, and she returns as "the good Fana," the woodland goddess of spring.

Whether we look at fire in its role of transforming a folkloric character such as Befana, or we view it as the life-renewing spirit of the land itself, its divine nature is always present. As humans we try to contain fire using a pit, a ring of stones, a lamp or a candle. Even though we may try and domesticate fire by placing it in a hearth, we can never remove its mystical nature. It is one that lures us into silent watchfulness as though we are awaiting some kind of answer, or listening to the inner whispers of an ancient spirit. Perhaps these are the voices of those who came before us.

The Ancestral Hearth

In mystical inner traditions, the hearth represents the ancient grotto, one of the earliest sites used by our ancestors for worship. The mantel symbolizes the ancient altars (once made of stone or wood) that were the center of veneration ceremonies. The chimney represents the gateway or passage between the worlds above and below. In this regard it shares a similar nature with Faery doors, which legend states are found in the hollows of old trees.

Because the hearth is associated with elements of ancient worship, and contains the sacred fire, it came to be regarded as a holy place in its own right. In effect it served to receive the prayers and offerings of the family and present or transfer them to the higher powers.

The hearth's nature of holiness generated many customs connecting to family life, tribe, and nation. One example is the giving of an oath before the fireplace. An oath sworn before the hearth was considered the most inviolable of all pledges. This practice ties in with the belief in the holiness of the heath and its living connection with the divine. To break an oath given at the hearth was to break the bond of trust with the gods themselves.

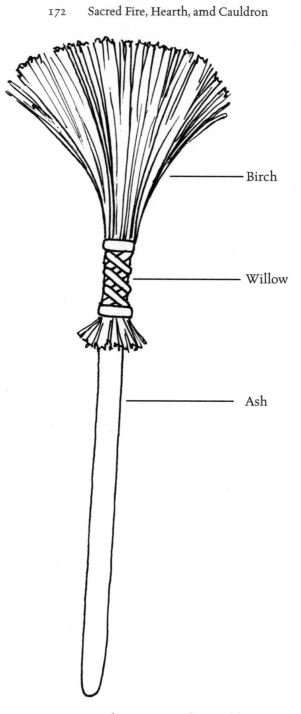

Birch

Willow

Ash

Figure 10: The Broom as the World Tree

As noted earlier, the hearth was attributed certain mystical and magical properties. It therefore follows that such qualities were transferred to the various tools associated with the hearth. One of the most important tools is the hearth broom. In occult tradition, the broom symbolizes feminine power and represents the goddess of the earth. Traditionally it is made of ash, birch, and willow. These trees all possess mystical associations connecting them with ancient themes of magic.

The ash tree often appears as the "World Tree" (a representation of the Universe). Wood and bark from the birch tree, in old folk lore, is said to wield power over the dead. The willow tree is sacred to Hecate, the goddess of the crossroads. This links the power of the "in-between" places to the hearth broom.

The assembly of the broom consists of the handle made of ash and the sweep made of thin birch branches, which are bound to the handle with strips of peeled willow bark. These woods also create a triformis nature to the broom, which grants it power over the three worlds.

As a magical tool, the broom is manipulated in specific ways. In the illustrations provided in this section you will note that the position of the broom links it to a specific nature. These postures help serve to activate occult forces. Through them, you can evoke and banish in ritual as well as in any work of magic. You can also tap into and draw forces of a celestial and chthonic nature.

EXERCISE NINE: *Awakening the Broom*

The exercise of awakening the broom connects you to the power of the sacred land and to Otherworld forces. The energy collected through this exercise can be used to enhance your creative magical power. Once established you can then channel the power into circle casting, ritual gesturing, charging objects, and other works of manifestation.

To begin, stand with the broom handle pointing down and touching the ground. Press down on the broom handle firmly and feel contact with the ground. Now visualize roots growing from the handle and penetrating deep down into the earth. Spend a moment with this visualization.

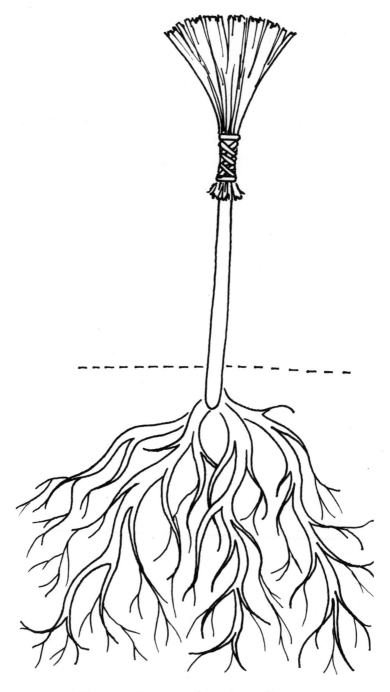

Figure 11: Broom with Underworld Roots

After a few moments of visualizing the roots, stop and imagine them spreading in all directions. Next, grasp the broom handle on its center with both hands and then take in a deep breath. As you do, *feel* the sensation of drawing the roots up toward you from below. As you sense this, slowly raise the broom with both hands, bringing them to your solar plexus. At this center, visualize a spiral of blue light swirling clockwise over the solar plexus. Next, visualize it entering your heart zone and merging with your body. Spend a few moments imagining that you are hollow and filled with blue light that will empower your magic. You can now proceed with ritual or magical broom work.

EXERCISE TEN: *Evoking Forces and Entities*

The broom can be used to evoke forces and entities. It can also be used to release, direct, or banish them. Prior to using the prescribed method you must always awaken the broom as in the previous exercise.

Once the broom is activated you can then wield it to attract. Focus your intent and then verbally declare what it is you want to evoke for ritual or magical purposes. For example, you might say, "I *evoke you, spirits of the moon*" or "I *evoke you, goddess of the moon.*" After declaring your intention, point the brush end of the broom downward and simply begin moving it in a clockwise manner. The motion is like stirring a cauldron with a large spoon. While you do this, say the following words:

> *From east, south, west and north,*
> I *summon, stir, and call you forth.*

Repeat the words along with the circling of the broom three times. If desired you can cast a circle using this method by simply walking along as you mark the area of the ritual circle. This is a traditional technique used in arcane forms of witchcraft.

The broom can also be used to banish or release. To use the broom in this way simply reverse the process of evocation. Focus your intent and then verbally declare that you wish to release what you evoked. For example, you might say: "I *release the energy of attachment, and bid farewell*

Figure 12A: Broom in Active Motion for Ritual and Magic

to you, spirits of the moon," or "I release the attachment of energy and bid fare-well to you, goddess of the moon." For times when force is required (instead of requested), you will use the word "banish."

After declaring your intention to release or banish, point the brush end of the broom downward and simply begin moving it in a counter-clockwise manner (using the same circular stirring motion). While you do this, say the following words:

To east, south, west, and north,
I summon, stir, and send you forth.

End by declaring the manifestation of your will. This is performed as in fig. 12B. Lift the broom up above your head, take in a deep breath, and feel yourself fill with power from above, below, and all directional quarters (singularly and in that order).

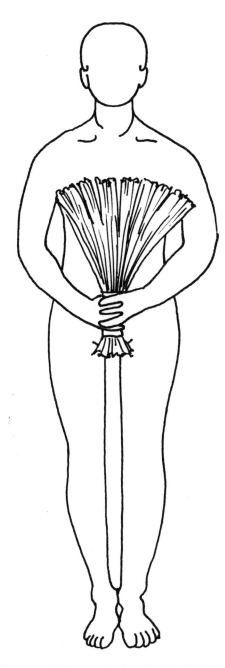

Figure 12B: Broom in Beginning Position

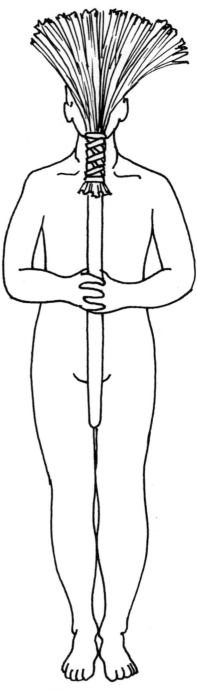

Figure 12C: Broom in Center Position

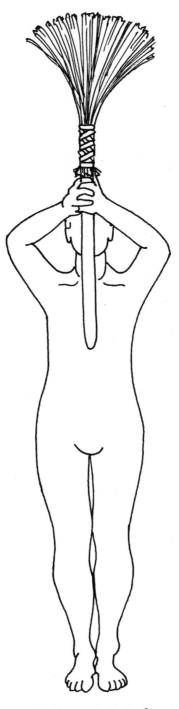

Figure 12D: Broom in Raised Position

Once you feel empowered, pull the broom downward with authority, saying the following words (and then slam the tip of the handle firmly on the ground as a point of exclamation):

As I declare, so mote it be!

EXERCISE ELEVEN: *Balancing Overworld and Underworld Powers*

Another method of evocation involves drawing celestial and chthonic forces with the broom. This establishes a balance of Overworld and Underworld powers, which are joined with elemental forces for significant works of magic and ritual. The process is similar to the other exercises but requires a slight variation. Various uses for this technique are described in the last chapter.

To begin, position the broom with the brush side up and the tip of the broom handle touching the ground. Grasp the handle midway with both hands and then slowly raise it up over your head.

Hold the broom overhead and visualize rays of the sun descending to touch the brush. Visualize a golden glow forming and then being absorbed into the brush. Next, visualize the moon sending rays of light that form a silver sphere, which is also absorbed. Last, visualize a starry night sky. Imagine seven stars appearing on the brush, which are then absorbed as well.

The next phase is to lower the broom back down until the handle touches the ground. At this point you perform the steps of awakening the broom as you did in exercise one. Following this, raise the broom with both hands until it reaches your solar plexus. Visualize a blue spiral forming and then entering your solar plexus area.

After visualizing the blue spiral, raise the broom up and "stir" the air in a clockwise manner, saying:

Powers of sun, moon, and shining star
I call to you, come from afar.

Next, reverse the broom position, brush end down, and lower it until it touches the floor. Then move the broom in a circular clockwise fashion, and say:

Powers below, of the secret race,
I call you now to this time and space."

Upon completion, stop and move both hands to the end of the handle and position them about six inches short of the tip. Once in position, use both hands to pivot the handle so that the brush end moves up and points away from you at solar plexus height. If done correctly, the tip of the broom handle points at your solar plexus and the broom is parallel to the ground with the brush facing in the opposite direction (away from you).

With the broom extended outward, move around to face each of the four directions (beginning with the east). As you move, with the brush end of the broom facing each cardinal point, say these words:

I call the forces that here surround,
And join above and below with all around.

End with the "exclamation of authority" broom manipulation from exercise two. In summary, you will raise and lower the broom, and when the tip forcefully connects with the ground, you say:

As I declare, so mote it be!

The Cauldron

In days of old, the hearth and the cauldron were inseparable. On a mundane level, the cauldron cooked the food, turning raw ingredients into complete meals. On a spiritual level, the cauldron serves as a model for transformation itself. The soup of the physical cauldron and the brew of the spiritual cauldron are nourishments of the two worlds.

Within the mystery tradition, the cauldron is both a vessel and a state of consciousness. It is the means and the end. In myth and legend, the cauldron is tended by nine muses, beings that bestow vision and enlightenment. This tells us that there are nine keys that unlock the door leading to enlightenment. *Nine* is the mystical number of the moon.

In astrology, the first crescent of the moon appears shortly after the dark moon/new moon (when the sun and moon are in conjunction). In the inner mysteries, the foam forming on the cauldron's brew symbolizes the new moon crescent. When the foam completely covers the bubbling brew, it then represents the full moon. At the time of the full moon, the sun and moon are in opposition (on opposite sides). In this state the brew is complete, and even just three drops is enough to create a Bard of unsurpassed wisdom and knowledge.

To become a bard of this rank one must race from the procreative darkness of the moon (when it is unseen in the night sky for *three* days) and taste the first emanation of light. The number three represents the principle of balance (the center point separating and maintaining the two opposites that flank it). Only when opposites are held in balance can enlightenment take place. In occult tradition, this teaching is represented by the three legs of the traditional cauldron.

As a vessel of enlightenment, the cauldron is sometimes referred to as the "Well of the Moon." This originates from an old witchcraft tradition in which the reflection of the full moon on a lake was known by this same title. Legend held that one must go to the Well of the Moon once every month. The Welsh lake known as Ffynnon Lloer was attached to a similar legend.

In Celtic lore the three daughters of Beag, son of Buan (of the Tuatha de Danaan), tended a mystical vessel called the Well of the Moon. It was from this vessel that the hero Fionn (or Finn) gained his skill with poetry and mastered its three levels. He also drank a second time and received the ability to foresee the future.

In old lore, the Well of the Moon, like the hidden cauldron itself, is chthonic in nature. It is found beneath the sea where it is fed by seven rivers. These rivers flow to and from the Well of the Moon. The number "seven" reflects the weekly cycle of the moon. The rivers of the Well of the Moon that fill and empty the vessel are a metaphor for the powers of the waxing and waning light of the moon.

Although the three daughters who guard the Well of the Moon are not mentioned as being blind, it is a common theme for cauldron guardians to have no physical sight. One example is in the tale of Ceridwen's cauldron, and another appears in the myth of Perseus who encounters three blind women guarding a cauldron. In the tale of Perseus the sisters share a magical sphere that grants vision to the holder.

The theme of blindness in the cauldron guardian is a metaphor of the three nights of the dark moon when it cannot be seen in the sky. This is the time of mystical versus mundane vision. It is, in effect, the inner sight of those who dwell in the Underworld or Otherworld of myth and legend. This is one reason that oracle powers are assigned to these hidden realms and why spirits of the dead are called upon to foretell the future.

You will find that performing cauldron work during the dark moon is particularly effective. This is connected to the occult theme of power in odd numbers (in this case the three nights of the dark moon). One very old connection to cauldron magic involves the use of a cauldron chain with twenty-five links. The symbolism of this chain reflects the power of five, and in this case it is five times five (the ultimate power of five). In numerology the number twenty-five is added to itself (2+5) to produce seven, which as we have seen is the number of the weekly cycle of the moon. In the system of numerology the number seven indicates completion.

The chain of twenty-five links was used to call spirits of the dead. This involved placing one hand on the chimney of the hearth, which as previously noted was believed to be the portal to the realm of the dead. The other hand was used to slide the fingers along each chain link, counting them off in groups of five (similar to the way a rosary is manipulated).

Because the number five is often regarded as indicating strife or unrest, it was used in cauldron magic to call spirits that had died a violent or unjust death. Such spirits were believed to seek vengeance, and were therefore good allies to use against enemies. In cauldron magic they are evoked down the chimney, out through the hearth opening, and into the cauldron.

The method of evocation required a specific designation. Therefore the prescribed invocation was spoken while counting off the chain links, as follows:

> I call upon the spirits of the dead who are at unrest. Come and feel avenged for the wrongs done to you. I call five spirits who were hanged, five who were tortured, five who were strangled, five who were burned, five who were crushed.

Once evoked, the spirits were then directed against an enemy, which often meant using a poppet doll or a clay image of the target person.

I do not encourage you to work with troubled spirits in this way, but you can call upon benevolent spirits using the basics of this old technique. To do so, simply change the wording to something more positive in nature. You can call spirits in general, using this technique for oracle purposes, or as a means of liberating trapped spirits. The latter is discussed in chapter thirteen.

It is my hope that this chapter has provided you with some insights into the mystical and magical setting of the hearth, its cauldron, and sacred fire. The core of what this all reflects is also the enchanted world in which our ancestors labored and celebrated. It is a part worth knowing and appreciating.

Now we approach the final chapters. Here you will find the presentation of the spiritual path associated with cauldron work as given in this book. Let us look now at the ways of the Cauldron Keeper.

THIRTEEN

WALKING THE PATH OF THE
CAULDRON KEEPER

Ancient myths and legends tell of Cauldron Guardians and Cauldron Keepers. In these stories the two roles are most commonly regarded as one and the same. However, for the purposes of this book they are not looked upon in this manner. In this chapter we will examine the role of the Cauldron Keeper and his or her spiritual and magical work.

The Cauldron Keeper is, in effect, a mystical Bard in the ancient sense. Bards, in days of old, were the preservers of knowledge and lore. In addition to this they were spiritual healers, a work performed through poetry, storytelling, and music.

In ancient myth we find that Hermes was the inventor of the harp (lyre) and the flute. In this sense we can connect him with the work of the Bard and consider him a patron deity. In addition, Hermes is associated with the crossroads, a place between the worlds. This liminal area is the true dwelling place of the mystical Bard.

An interesting side note to this is the urban legend of the blues musician at the crossroads. According to the tale, a musician seeking great skill, fame, and fortune sells his soul to the Devil at the crossroads. The Devil is always a trickster spirit, which identifies him with Hermes. This is especially so (in keeping with this legendary reference) when we factor in the musical connection to Hermes of the crossroads.

One of the duties of the Bard is to fend off the influence of trickster spirits by guarding against distortion, deception, and falsehoods. This, of course, is reflected in the Bard's role as a true preserver of knowledge and teachings.

The Way of the Cauldron Keeper

The work of the Cauldron Keeper involves several categories. If you choose to become a Cauldron Keeper, then the following list will guide you in walking the path:

- The Magical Craft
- Healing
- Spiritual Development
- Ancestral Veneration
- Cord Work
- Sacred Tree Cords and Prayer
- Daily Alignment

In this section we will explore each of these categories and examine the particulars as they pertain to the ways of the Cauldron Keeper. Presented in each grouping is the prescribed method of operation. You can personalize this to suit you, but I recommend adhering to the given basic structure as closely as possible. Feel free, however, to include additional practices in your shamanic approach.

The Magical Craft

A Cauldron Keeper believes in limitless potential, and because this is the core definition of magic, the keeper also believes in the art of magic. Cauldron magic consists of what is called "raised power" and "drawn power" (or a combination of both). The former refers to an inherent inner personal power, and the latter refers to energy that is attracted from an outside source.

For the purposes of this chapter, we will work with the concept known as the *Mist of Enchantment*. The mist is an etheric energy produced in inner cauldron work. The mist possesses the magical property to instill or to remove. In other words, we can add a magical intent to one thing, or we can dissolve away a preexisting condition.

In the beginning stages of cauldron work you will need a physical cauldron. Its size is unimportant, but I recommend that you use one at least about the size of a large orange. Make sure it is made of a metal that can be heated without melting or cracking. Once you are experienced in cauldron work you will no longer require a material one, but personally I prefer to use a physical cauldron.

To prepare for cauldron work, fill it halfway with sand. If sand is not available you can use potting soil. Obtain a feather that is large enough to fan the cauldron smoke away from the vessel (an owl feather is traditional). You will also need three candles (minimum six inches long): one red, one black, and one white. Place them around the cauldron so that they form a triangle enclosing the cauldron in its center.

The top point of the triangle indicates whether you are sending or receiving the mist. Place the point facing you when desiring to receive, and pointing away when wishing to transmit to someone else. The colored candles are always set with the red candle marking the top point of the triangle. The base of the triangle is marked with the white candle on the right side and the black on the left. Therefore you will need to arrange the orientation of the candles in accord with your intent.

The final component of cauldron work is called "informing" the magic. What this means is that you must *impregnate* the energy with a symbol of your intent or desire. This requires what is called a sigil, which is an image that represents what you want to manifest. Let us examine the means used to *inform* energy.

If I want to impregnate energy with the concept of healing, I can make a sigil to represent this intent. One method is take the word "heal," and turn it into an image by rearranging the letters. There are a variety of ways to do this, and this is where your imagination comes into play. You can overlap the letters, turn them in different directions, or whatever you decide. In the end you want the sigil to look nothing like a word at all. The only "rule" is that no single letter should be left not touching another.

Step 1.

Step 2.

Step 3.

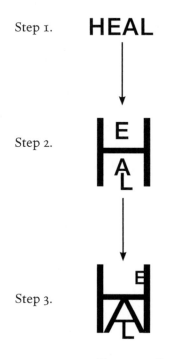

**Figure 13: Creating a Sigil by Transforming
the Letters of a Word**

To inform, begin by drawing your sigil on a piece of paper (parchment is traditional). It should be no larger than the palm of your hand. Once drawn out, hold it in your right hand and declare the intent. Using the example of healing, you say: "I *inform this sigil with the intent to heal.*" Spend a few moments focusing your thoughts and *see* the successful outcome in your mind.

The next step is to light a charcoal block and set it on the sand inside your cauldron. If you are indoors do not use the type of charcoal made for the barbecue as its smoke is very toxic and potentially deadly. Use instead a self-igniting charcoal, which is commonly sold in New Age and Earth Religion shops for the purpose of burning powdered and resin incense.

When the charcoal appears to be burning look intently at the sigil. Focus only on its form, and do not think about what it means or represents. Your subconscious mind is processing that and is connecting with astral levels that will help build the power of the "formed-thought" as you continue working.

The next phase is to visualize the inner cauldrons taking shape within your body zones. Begin with the Cauldron of Regeneration at the base or genital zone. See it form with your mind's eye. Imagine that you are looking down at the opening of the mouth of the cauldron. Mentally picture a dark liquid that has filled it.

Visualize the sigil appearing on the surface of the dark liquid. If you have difficulty with this you can look at the sigil and then press it against the area of your body containing the inner cauldron. But ideally you should obtain the visualization. The next step is to visualize the sigil sinking into the liquid and disappearing. When this is accomplished, say a conjuration like the following:

> By *blood, bone, metal, and fire,*
> *set into motion what I desire.*

Move your attention to your solar plexus and visualize the Cauldron of Abundance forming there. Repeat the process of visualizing the sigil on the liquid surface, and then sinking into the cauldron. Once it has, say the conjuration:

> By *blood, metal, fire, and bone,*
> *Bring to life what I have sown.*

Focus now on the area of your head. Visualize the Cauldron of Enlightenment forming here. Repeat the entire process with the sigil and the liquid as you did before with the other cauldrons. Finish with the invocation:

> By *blood, fire, bone, and metal,*
> *cauldron steam and magic settle.*

To complete the final phase, drop the paper with the sigil on top of the charcoal. As the smoke rises, fan it with the feather (away from you for sending, and toward you for receiving) and say the incantation:

The cauldron's mist that here I see
is now the thing so named by me.

It is at this point that you state precisely what you seek to manifest. In the case of healing, you can say: "I *name you the power to heal*" or "I *name you healer of* ___" (give the proper name of the illness or condition). Once you have named the mist, you must perform one last procedure in order to set the power. You will need something to bind the energy to, such as a bottle of essential oil or a metal or stone item. These materials hold a charge better and longer than resin.

Place the selected item in your left hand (or if size and weight is a problem, then rest your hand on the object). Visualize the three inner cauldrons resting at each body center. Next, visualize the top cauldron moving down and the bottom cauldron moving upward, to where the two merge into the center cauldron, becoming one single cauldron.

Visualize the cauldron glowing with blue light. The light then forms into a stream of vaporous mist that rises upward. Take a deep breath in through your nose and imagine the mist swirling in your chest area. Hold the imagery and your breath for a moment. As you exhale slowly, visualize the blue mist flowing out within your breath. Direct your breath into the bottle of oil (or see it pass into the object you have chosen).

As you become more familiar with cauldron magic you can enhance or modify the techniques. One example is to add non-toxic herbs to the paper sigil on the charcoal, and then inhale the smoke as it rises from the cauldron. This smoke is then exhaled outward to send the mist, or exhaled down into the oil (or on the object) to set the energy.

Oil that has been charged with the enchanted mist can be worn so as to absorb the magical intent. A charged object such as a metal ring with a stone can be worn for the same results. A metal necklace will serve the same purpose.

Previously, I mentioned that the enchanted mist can also remove something. This is accomplished in a different way, although most of the procedure is identical to manifesting the mist. To begin: take the cauldron, remove all of the sand, and fill the vessel halfway with water. You will place the cauldron over a fire, so make sure that the material it is made of can withstand the heat. If not, you can use a metal cooking pan, but ideally you should obtain a cauldron that can be directly heated.

Light a white utility candle, and place a plastic bottle cap on your work area. The cap should be the type that is typically found on a bottle of drinking water. Position the cap so that it can be filled like a cup. With the cap upright, tilt the lighted candle over it so that the melting wax fills it. This will take a minute or two, and during the process it is helpful to turn and roll the candle with your fingers.

When the cap is filled with wax, let it cool and harden. You can speed this up by putting it in the refrigerator for at least twenty minutes. Once the wax is hard, take a toothpick (or some other item) and pry the wax from the cap (scrape and carve all along the inside edge of the cap). When the wax disk is free, you can etch the sigil into the wax with the toothpick (or use a permanent marking pen to draw it on the wax). The sigil needs to represent the thing you want to remove.

When the wax sigil is ready, "inform" it as in the previous example. As before, you will hold it in your right hand and declare the intent. This is followed by a declaration such as "I *inform this sigil with the intent to remove bad luck*." Spend a few moments focusing your thoughts and *see* the successful outcome in your mind (picture what you wish removed and then what you want to replace it).

Heat the cauldron so that the water will boil. While it heats, sit comfortably in preparation for the cauldron work ahead. Visualize the Cauldron of Regeneration forming at your genital area. Picture the view as looking down at the open mouth of the cauldron. Visualize the dark liquid filled to the top.

Picture the sigil appearing on the surface of the dark liquid, and then visualize it sinking into the liquid where it then disappears. When this is accomplished, say a conjuration like the following:

By *blood, bone, metal, and fire,*
Remove this thing of no desire.

Now, focus your attention on your solar plexus and visualize the Cauldron of Abundance forming there. Repeat the process of visualizing the sigil on the liquid surface, and then sinking into the cauldron. Once it has, say the conjuration:

By *blood, metal, fire, and bone,*
Wither away what fate has sown.

Move your attention now to the area of your head. Visualize the Cauldron of Enlightenment forming here. Repeat the entire process with the sigil and the liquid as you did before with the other cauldrons. Finish with the invocation:

By *blood, fire, bone, and metal,*
cauldron steam, magic unsettle.

To complete the final phase, drop the wax sigil into the cauldron of boiling water. As the steam rises, fan it with the feather to send it away, and say the incantation:

The cauldron's mist that here I see,
remove the thing so named by me.

As before, state precisely what you want to happen. In the example of bad luck you can say: "I *name you bad luck*" or "I *name you* _____" (state the condition itself).

The rest of the process resembles what you performed earlier. Visualize the three inner cauldrons resting at each body center. Mentally move the top cauldron down and the bottom cauldron upward. Merge the two cauldrons with the center one and visualize them all becoming one single cauldron.

*Cauldron of
Enlightenment*

3. Visualize having what you desire.

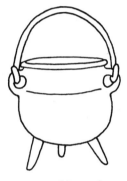

*Cauldron of
Abundance*

2. Envision the feeling of what you desire
   (how would it change anything?).

*Cauldron of
Regeneration*

1. Dissolve the image of anything preventing
   what you desire. See it turn into mist and
   disappear into the cauldron.

Figure 14: Cauldrons

Visualize the inner cauldron glowing with blue light. Picture the light forming into a stream of vaporous mist that rises upward. Take a deep breath in through your nose and imagine the mist swirling in your chest area. Hold the imagery and your breath for a moment. As you exhale slowly, visualize the blue mist flowing out within your breath. Direct your breath into the steam of the boiling cauldron.

Finish by watching the water boil away until it is completely evaporated. Afterward, remove the cauldron from the fire and let it cool thoroughly before handling it. When the cauldron is completely cool again, cleanse it with soap and water, dry it thoroughly, and put it away.

You can perform other works of cauldron magic by applying the basic formula of manifestation. Begin by sitting in the cauldron posture. Visualize the Cauldron of Regeneration forming at your genital area, and then think about the things that block you from what you desire to manifest. Next, transform this into a symbol (or at least a simple singular image). Then speak the following words as you visualize the symbol or image disintegrating into a dark mist:

I *dissolve that which blocks my desire, and* I *remove its attachment to me on the material plane.*

Now, visualize the dark mist descending into the Cauldron of Regeneration. Picture it disappearing into the bubbling brew. Then say these words:

I *purify the energy of this mist.* I *neutralize and remove its intention, purpose, and function. It is now pure uncontaminated energy without an informed intent.*

Visualize the energy rising from the cauldron as a glowing sphere of blue light. Spend a few moments with this imagery. Next, visualize the Cauldron of Abundance forming at your solar plexus. Bring the blue sphere to this cauldron and allow it to hover it over the opening.

Focus your mind on the blue sphere and say:

I pass into this sphere my desire to manifest [name it] *in my life.*

Now concentrate on the essence of what you desire without picturing it. For example, if you want money for travel, think instead of how it would feel to have the freedom to travel. Transfer this by visualizing the sphere changing into a color that represents the essence of your desire. Some examples are gold for money, red for passion, pink for friendship, green for healing, orange for good luck, and blue for peace. Once you have pictured the color, visualize the sphere of light moving down into the cauldron and disappearing.

The next step is to visualize the Cauldron of Enlightenment taking form around your head area. Imagine the colored sphere rising from it and hovering above the cauldron. Focus on this and say these words:

I *manifest what* I *desire.*

Finish by visualizing precisely what you want to manifest. If you want money, for example, then see yourself with lots of cash or a large bank deposit in your favor. But bear in mind that magic does not create cash out of thin air. It works through the path of least resistance. This means it will come to you in the only way it reasonably can. This may happen through an inheritance from someone dying in the family or from an insurance settlement from a personal injury. Always think this through before calling on magic to manifest your desires. It is advisable to specify the means through which the money will come into your hands.

Healing with the Cauldron

The Cauldron Keeper should live the healthiest lifestyle possible in accord with his or her personal needs. Being in good health yourself is a precondition for performing healing work on others. This is because, in part, you are passing some of your vital energy into the person you are healing. In addition, you are also in contact with the energy of the illness you are treating, and for this reason you need to possess good health as a resistance against contaminating your own aura. Take note that disease always forms in the aura before it manifests in the body.

As part of the healing work, you will be using visualizations of the inner cauldrons. The use of the inner cauldron for the purpose of healing involves the addition and the removal of energy within the body's centers of power. You will be pouring healing energy into the inner cauldrons as well as displacing and neutralizing the energy of ill health. This is, in essence, a cleansing technique as well as a means of regeneration.

The manifestation of illness is also an elemental imbalance in the sense that there is either an excess or lack of one or more elemental energies at play. The four elements of earth, air, fire, and water are creative forces. Unfortunately they can create illness as well as health, so we must use the balancing energy of the fifth element as well, which is the element of spirit.

Before beginning any healing work, the illness needs to be classified as belonging to one or more elemental natures. In addition, you will identify the section of the body with an element as well. This will determine what energies you need to deal with regarding the illness and where its root source is located.

The body itself can be divided into four elemental sections. The head, neck, and lungs are associated with air. The heart, digestive system, and vital organs belong to water. The reproductive system is assigned to fire, and the legs and feet are of earth. The arms and hands are also assigned to the earth element. In general, the illness will be associated with the elemental force that alters the cohesion of the elemental energy force in the body zone. For example, water changes the cohesion of earth, fire affects air and water (and vice versa). Therefore think about what is showing up in the symptoms. This will give you an idea of which elements you are dealing with. Let's look at some examples.

Illnesses of the lungs, neck, and head/brain are adversely affecting the elemental nature of air in the corresponding areas of the body. If the symptoms are associated with such things as excessive or unusual mucus, swelling, or bleeding, then the element of water is creating a problem.

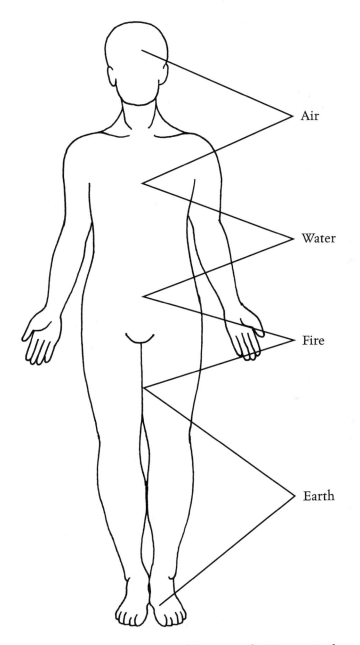

Figure 15: Elemental Zones in the Human Body

Health issues involving the heart, digestive tract, and vital organs are affecting the elemental nature of water in this body zone. If the symptoms are related to constriction, spasms, or circulation, then an earth imbalance is at work.

When the affected part of the body involves the reproductive organs, then something is adversely working against the element of fire. When the symptoms include infection, irritation, and excessive urges, it is a sign of an air imbalance.

Physical problems with the legs, knees, ankles, feet, and arm parts show up due to an earth imbalance. Adverse symptoms like breaks, stiffness, and weakness are indications of a water imbalance.

Elemental imbalances can do one of two things. They can create an overabundance of one element. For example, too much elemental water can cause the earth element to expand. The other thing that can happen is a diminishment of an element. This can show up when too much fire enters into elemental air. Ideally, we want all the elemental natures to be proportionally equal, supportive, and harmonious toward one another.

Some diseases have elemental associations themselves, and this is another elemental nature we need to take into consideration for healing work. Cancer, for example is essentially a fire-based element. Earth and water are effective elements to work with against cancer, while the element of air is one that requires discernment in finding an appropriate approach.

To determine the elemental nature of a disease or illness, give some thought to how it operates. Its actions are the keys to understanding the elements at work (and some diseases have more than one elemental nature). Because this can be complicated, I have devised for you a method of elemental healing work that will serve you until you come to learn more through your own research and experience. The instructions are part of the overall process that follows in this section.

Begin the preparation for healing work by visualizing a five-pointed star. Trace this in the air over the person's body, making it large enough to encompass him or her. Once traced out, picture the top point of the star, and then place the palms of both hands over the area of the body that needs healing (for systemic conditions, position one hand over the head and the other over the feet). Now, sound out the tonal of elemental spirit: *Ummmm…oooh.*

Next, make the sound of each elemental nature in the following order as you visualize a spiral turning clockwise:

Water: Oooo

Fire: Iiii

Air: Eeee

Earth: Aaaa

Finish by visualizing the large five-pointed star glowing. Once you have this image clearly in your mind's eye visualize it condensing inward as it enters the person's body at the solar plexus. This is the area in which the astral body receives its energy. Once the star is absorbed into the body, visualize the body glowing as did the star before it entered. Hold this visualization for a few moments.

To begin the next phase, have the patient sit comfortably in front of you (you will be facing each other). Visualize your Cauldron of Regeneration forming at the genital area. Ask the patient to visualize their own cauldron forming as well. As they do this, take in three deep breaths and visualize each one filling your inner cauldron with blue light.

Once your cauldron has received the third breath of light, magically *inform* it with the pertinent imagery of intention (as outlined in the section on the magical craft). Once the energy is informed, cup your hands together at your genital area as though you are keeping water in your hands. Visualize the blue light rising from the cauldron and pouring into your hands. With your cupped hands filled with blue light, move them over to the patient and mentally pour the light into their inner cauldron. Guide the person through the visualization with words such as:

I want you to visualize a glowing blue liquid of healing energy pouring from my hands into your cauldron and filling it to the rim.

Here you will need to use your intuition and imagination as required to aid the patient through this imagery in case he or she struggles with the process.

Once the patient's inner cauldron is filled, you will then visualize your Cauldron of Abundance forming at your solar plexus area. Direct the patient to visualize his or her own forming as well. Now, using the three breaths method, along with the blue light technique, fill the inner Cauldron of Abundance as you did for the Cauldron of Regeneration (and *inform* it). Once filled, cup your hands to receive the light as before, and pour it into the patient's cauldron (guiding them to receive the blue liquid light as with the previous cauldron).

It now remains to visualize the inner Cauldron of Enlightenment forming around your head area. Use the breathing and blue light sequence as before in the case of the other two inner cauldrons (and remember to *inform* the energy). Once filled, carry the light from your cauldron and pass it into the patient's Cauldron of Enlightenment. You will guide them through this process as needed.

The last phase is to integrate the three inner cauldrons with the patient's body. Begin by focusing on the top cauldron and direct the patient to think about his or her medical condition. Have the person name it, or give it a name (it is said out loud). Then have the patient think about the symptoms he or she is experiencing. Allow the patient a few moments of internal reflection before moving on to the next step.

Inform the patient that you are going to touch his or her forehead with your fingertips, and then do so. Guide the patient through the following visualization by speaking words such as these to the patient:

Where my fingers touch is the inner Cauldron of Enlightenment. It is filled with healing energy that empowers your mind. Say to yourself, "I send the message to my entire body to eliminate disharmony and restore equilibrium"…now visualize the cauldron tipping and pouring out the blue light, which flows down into the cauldron at your solar plexus. Feel the blue healing light flowing down your body.

Lightly drag your fingertips down from the forehead, moving from the face to the neck, and down across the exact center of the chest, coming to rest on the solar plexus.

With light pressure on the solar plexus, guide the patient through the following visualization by speaking words such as these to him or her:

> *Where my fingers touch is the inner Cauldron of Abundance. It is filled with healing energy that empowers your emotions. Say to yourself, "I send the message to my entire being to eliminate disharmony and restore equilibrium"….now visualize the cauldron tipping and pouring out the blue light, which flows down into the cauldron at your base center. Feel the blue healing light flowing down your body.*

Lightly drag your fingertips down from the solar plexus, moving from the chest to the navel, and down across the belly to just above the pubic area, coming to rest there.

Press lightly on this area and guide the patient through the following visualization by speaking words such as these to him or her:

> *Where my fingers touch is the inner Cauldron of Regeneration. It is filled with healing energy that empowers your biology. Say to yourself, "I send the message to my entire being to eliminate disharmony and restore equilibrium"…now visualize the cauldron expanding outward. See it grow larger…and larger…it is now so large that you are sitting inside of it. Become aware of your body frame and feel the cauldron around you.*

Place the palms of your hands on the patient, one on the right arm and the other on the left. Once in place, say: "*You are contained within the healing cauldron.*" Direct the patient to visualize himself/herself glowing as a being of blue light. Allow the patient a few minutes to remain with this imagery. Keep your hands in place.

The last phase is to empower the patient with elemental healing energy. Remove your hands and instruct the patient to visualize the cauldron fading away and disappearing (affirm to the patient that it has done its work and is dissolving away, taking none of its healing energy with it). Have him or her place their palms on the floor, and then inhale and exhale deeply and slowly three times. Do this with the patient, as it will help ground you as well.

Inform the patient that you will now channel elemental energy to aid in the healing process. Direct the person to inhale slowly in and out whenever you say the name of one of the four elements. Lastly, instruct the patient to repeat these words after you (be sure to speak slowly and wait for the patient to follow as he or she will take a breath within each sentence):

I call upon air to disperse the clouds of illness within me. They go away completely.

I call upon fire to burn away the illness within me. It is completely vanquished.

I call upon water to cleanse and carry away the remains of illness within me. Illness is completely washed away.

I call upon earth to fortify my body, mind, and emotions against illness within me. Illness cannot prevail against me.

You can change the word "illness" to "injury" or "disease," as well as modify the sentence to suit each case. The important thing is to reinforce that the problem is dissolved away and removed, and that it cannot return to overtake the patient.

Spiritual Development

The ancient tales of mystical cauldrons are, at heart, stories of personal transformation. The Cauldron Keeper incorporates this theme in order to work on his or her spiritual development and evolution. In this way the stories of lost or hidden cauldrons speak to the journey of the soul through various lifetimes within the material realm.

Spiritual transformation is a process of discovery and integration. In the cauldron tales, the hero is always in pursuit of that which is lost or hidden. As a metaphor, the hidden realm of the cauldron is that part of our spirit that is lost to the realm of physical existence. This is because, in part, the sensory stimulation of material existence pushes the indwelling spirit into the inner recesses of the vessel it inhabits.

When we consider the reincarnated soul, in context with the tale of the lost cauldron, we note that, in the majority of cases, past lives appear to be forgotten. Just as the hero must journey in search of the cauldron, so too must a personal effort be made to retrieve past life memories. Where the legendary cauldron seeker must enter the Underworld, the past life seeker must enter the subconscious realm of nonmaterial reality.

The recollection of past lives can be useful in understanding our current lifetime experience. Past lives shape who we are now, and the condition of our lives, just as do the stages in this lifetime when we were six years old, twelve, twenty-one, and so on. We are a culmination of every decade we have lived. Through them our experiences and our reactions have shaped the person we have come to be.

But does it help us in any practical way to remember being twelve or twenty years old? Does it help us now to know who we were centuries ago? If you knew who you were in 1546, would it change anything in your life today? The answer is "probably not" but it may help you to understand the challenges you now encounter. This is related to the idea of energy attachment as in the notion of karma.

The basic idea of karma is one of *cause and effect*, although some people view karma as a reward-and-punishment system. This idea holds that the condition of your current life is a direct result of your actions and attitudes within a previous life. According to such a view, the good things in your present life are rewards and the bad things are punishments.

The Cauldron Keeper views all of this in a different light. The keeper regards past life experiences as energy that attaches to the soul. It forms the foundation of the aura field of energy that surrounds our material body. The energy does not exist for the purpose of reward or punishment, but it does attract compatible energy to itself. If your spiritual vibration is positive in nature, then you will attract things (and people) that share the same or similar vibration. The same principle is at work when the spiritual vibration is negative. This is the magical principle of "like attracts like."

Inner cauldron work can be used to cleanse the energy field of negative attachments. It can also be used to enhance the aura with positive vibrations. This is an important aspect of the basic spiritual approach of the Cauldron Keeper. Another element is the generation of *informed* energy, which is created to establish new patterns of energy that can reshape the life condition.

The basic concept of spiritual cauldron work is to view the three inner cauldrons as modifiers. In this light the Cauldron of Regeneration influences overall vitality. The Cauldron of Abundance affects the emotional state. The Cauldron of Enlightenment influences mentality. Let us look at each quality.

The Cauldron of Regeneration

The vitality of our lives is core to the passion we bring to the life we live. It is the generator and the empowering force of motivation. In some occult circles it is called the *fire of adolescence*. The word "adolescent" is ultimately derived from the Latin *alescere*, which means to nourish. In the common definition, adolescence is the period between youth and maturity. Therefore it is the in-between place, which in previous chapters we have noted is the most magical of all. The fire of adolescence is neither the naivety of childhood nor the tainted condition of maturity. It is instead the fire of limitless potentiality. Through the Cauldron of Regeneration we are reminded that anything is possible.

The Cauldron of Abundance

The emotional state of our lives is what provides balance. In this light, balance is inner peace. This is a state that exists in between the natures of receptivity and reaction. It generates no objection or conflict outward into the lives of other people.

But when balance is not present, then the emotional state becomes one of questioning, objecting, and confronting. It does this because it desires the restoration of inner peace, and so it seeks to neutralize the outer stimulation that disturbed that peace. When our emotions are agitated we tend to call upon other people to modify their behavior so that we can return to our sense of peace. In this reaction we fail to realize that we have surrendered peace in the first place by allowing someone else to move us away from inner balance. The Cauldron of Abundance reminds us that we are responsible for our own harvest.

The Cauldron of Enlightenment

Our mentality is the filter through which we regard and judge. This serves to discern things and people outside of ourselves, but also tends to reflect our own inner makeup of character and nature. When we look at others we are often seeing an isolated representation of ourselves. Whether we like the image or hate it is often a matter of how we feel about ourselves.

People frequently use the expression "in light of this" or "in this light" to express how something modifies or changes perspective. Enlightenment is the quality that ultimately transforms judgment into something else. In a spiritual sense, we find that enlightened figures of the past, such as Jesus or Buddha, appear to operate without judging altogether.

The Cauldron of Enlightenment is influenced by the adolescent fire burning beneath the Cauldron of Regeneration, as well as the steam rising from the Cauldron of Abundance. Together they flavor the brew of enlightenment. But we must note that what stirs in the Cauldron of Enlightenment also affects the other two cauldrons. The three are actually one, which is why the exercises in cauldron work always include them together.

The way we regard life, and the people who share it with us, is rooted in what we brew within the three inner cauldrons of our spirituality. The good news is that we can add to this, subtract from it, or keep true to the recipe. The Cauldron of Enlightenment reminds us that we make the choices that affect the condition of our lives (even when we fail to choose, it is a choice to do nothing).

Spiritual Cleansing with the Cauldron

The inner cauldrons can be used to cleanse the aura and remove the daily contamination related to negative people and events. This is the simplest use of the cauldrons, but is still very beneficial. As with all cauldron work, you will call upon all three cauldrons.

One of the best ways of using the cauldrons for cleansing is to incorporate the process into your bath time. Once your bath water is ready, remain outside of the tub for a few moments. Imagine that the tub is a large mystical cauldron that has been set for you. Spend a moment with this thought.

Step into the water and pause while you visualize yourself standing in the enchanted cauldron. Once you have envisioned this, lower yourself down into the water and sit comfortably. Feel the warmth of the water and imagine that you are sitting in a cauldron heated by a mystical flame beneath it. Say these words of affirmation:

I am in the enchanted cauldron, whose waters purify and cleanse.

Close your eyes and visualize the inner Cauldron of Regeneration forming at your genital area. Using your hands in the water gently pull soft waves toward your belly and imagine that this water is filling the cauldron. Next, imagine a blue glow of light formed around the filled cauldron. As you look at it, the light turns into rising steam. Take a deep slow breath in and visualize the steam drawn up into your solar plexus, where it forms a spiral. Visualize the Cauldron of Abundance forming in this area. Imagine the spiral moving into the cauldron, where it disappears.

Focus your attention on the Cauldron of Abundance and visualize a blue sphere rising up from inside. Mentally move the sphere up to the area of your head. Visualize the Cauldron of Enlightenment forming. When this image is strong in your mind, lower the sphere over the cauldron. Imagine it glowing with blue light.

Visualize a fountain of water shooting up from the cauldron and cascading back down. Now, cup the bath water with both hands, scoop some of it up, and pour it over your head. Repeat this three times, and as you do, visualize the water from the fountain pouring down your body. Say these words of affirmation each time:

The cleansing water of the enchanted cauldron washes away all that is negative, imbalanced, and impure.

At this stage you can continue with bathing as usual. When you are finished, there is one last step. Unplug the tub and as the water begins to drain out, say these words of affirmation:

This water carries away all that is negative, imbalanced, and impure.

You do not need to remain while the bath drains.

Spiritual Enhancement Through Cauldron Work

To enhance your spiritual development the inner cauldrons can serve to inspire various traits. In Greco-Roman mythology the nine Muses watched over a mystical cauldron, and in Celtic lore we find a hidden cauldron tended by nine maidens of the Otherworld. This basic theme can be used in inner cauldron work.

Spiritual enhancements require a pathworking journey. To begin you will need to meditate on a spiritual quality that you want to enhance. Some examples are compassion, tolerance, generosity, truthfulness, devotion, service, and contentment. Choose a single trait for each individual pathworking. Write the name of the quality on a piece of paper and set it in your physical cauldron just prior to beginning the journey.

Start by visualizing a country road that crosses an open meadow and disappears into the woods. You are walking along the path and all around you are beautiful flowers in full bloom. You continue to walk as you approach the woods.

You are walking into the forest, following the road as it goes deeper into the trees. The trees are very old oaks that stand tall and straight. You sense that they have been this way since before humans were civilized. You continue to walk.

In the distance you see a clearing in the forest. You notice three large boulders that seem to mark the spot. You walk up to the rocks. As you approach, you find yourself on a hill that slopes gently down to a grotto. You feel compelled to move toward it.

You are close to the grotto now, and you see a cave within it. You approach the cave, but do not enter it. As you stand in front of the cave opening, you hear the sound of female voices whispering from inside. In a moment nine maidens appear and step out of the cave. You notice they are carrying a cauldron.

One of the maidens speaks to you: "*Why have you come to the Grotto of the Faeries?*" You reply, "*My journey is to strengthen my spirit.*" The maiden asks, "*And what this day will fulfill your Quest?*" You answer, "*I seek the enrichment of* [name the spiritual virtue]." The maiden smiles and says, "*Then you shall drink your fill of* [name virtue] *this day.*"

The maiden instructs you to sit in front of the cauldron and you comply. Three of the nine maidens approach the cauldron and pour a vial of liquid into it [*touch the area of your genitals with your left hand*]. One of the three maidens dips a ladle into the cauldron and puts it up to your mouth for you to drink from. You drink some of the liquid [*touch the thumb of your left hand to your lips*].

Another set of three maidens come forward and add their vial to the cauldron's brew [*touch your solar plexus with your left hand*]. One of the three maidens dips a ladle into the cauldron and puts it up to your mouth for you to drink from. You drink some of the liquid [*touch the thumb of your left hand to your lips*].

The last set of three maidens steps to the cauldron and pour their vial [*touch your forehead with your left hand*]. One of the three maidens dips a ladle into the cauldron and puts it up to your mouth for you to drink from. You drink some of the liquid [*touch the thumb of your left hand to your lips*].

The nine maidens form a circle around you and begin to dance. They start to hum a melody, but it quickly turns to the sound of bees all around you. You begin to feel as though you are falling asleep. You sit down to rest and find yourself dreaming [*now, in daydream style, imagine yourself as you might behave if you could fully express the spiritual trait you selected in this pathworking. Spend a few moments meditating on interacting with people or performing a task, etc.*].

When you are ready to close the pathworking episode, visualize the path leading up from the grotto to the hilltop. You are walking back up the hill. You reach the top and there you find three boulders. The path continues on the other side and leads into the woods. You move to the road and enter the forest.

As you walk along the path you notice tall towering oak trees all around you. These trees stand true and straight. You continue to walk along the road. In the distance you see the trees begin to thin, which reveals the sight of a meadow ahead.

You are walking along the path and it leaves the tree line. You are now on the road, walking through the meadow. Beautiful flowers surround you. You continue to walk. You find yourself back where you started on your journey.

Take in a deep breath and slowly exhale. Repeat this three times. Become aware of the sounds around you and feel the physical sensation of your body. You are now fully returned to this time and space.

This pathworking has connected you to the vibration of the virtue you wish to enhance. You must express it in some conscious and purposeful way in your life. Recall your dream in front of the grotto. How can you perform this, or some degree of it, in the material world over the next few days? Your task is to plan this and execute it. Once you do, then the virtue will take root in your spirit.

Ancestral Veneration

In a previous chapter we looked at the establishment of an ancestral shrine. You can add another dimension to veneration through a related cauldron operation. This incorporates the use of a physical cauldron, a skull representation, and an offering of food and drink.

Required items:

- A cauldron
- A skull representation
- A glass (to contain liquid)

- A plate or bowl (for food offering)
- A red candle and candle holder
- A bell
- Three dried beans (fava beans if possible)
- Food and drink: Ideally this should be something your ancestors (or specific relatives) would have enjoyed in their lifetime.

Begin by setting the cauldron as the center piece. Place the dried beans inside. Set the skull in front of the cauldron, and the candle in front of the skull. The bell is placed to the right of the cauldron, and the food and drink is arranged to the left.

Ring the bell three times, and then set it back down. Light the candle, raise it upright a few inches and pass it in front of the skull in a clockwise motion three times (you will be tracing a circle in the air, the skull in its center). While moving the candle, say:

I call through the dark veil with this light. I call to my ancestors [or someone specific]. Come and partake of my offering of food and drink.

Visualize a sphere of blue light appearing in the east quarter, which then moves above the skull and settles into it. Put the candle down to the right of the skull. Move the food and drink over in front of the skull. Ring the bell three times over the food and again over the drink. Set it back down again, place your palms over the food and drink, and say:

We are a circle that is unbroken in endless time. We are a circle that remains unbroken in endless time.

Pass the palm of your right hand over the food and drink in a clockwise circular motion three times. Then, with the fingers of your left hand, trace a circle clockwise around the areas of your inner cauldrons, beginning with the Cauldron of Regeneration and ending with the Cauldron of Enlightenment.

Allow several minutes to pass before bidding farewell to your ancestors. You can play music, sing, meditate, or even just remain in silent reverence. Bear in mind that this period of time is not appropriate for making requests. You can do this afterward just prior to the release.

When you are ready to complete everything, ring the bell three times. Next, raise the candle and say:

Beloved ancestors, it is time to bid farewell until we meet again. With love and in peace I request that you return now to your own realm.

Move the candle in a counter-clockwise circle, and visualize the blue sphere of light rising from the skull and departing (disappearing into the west quarter). Take the three dried beans out of the cauldron and set them with the food. Blow out the candle, remove everything, and clean up any debris.

Cord Work

The Cauldron Keeper has three sets of cords at his or her command. These are the White Serpent cord, the Spirit cord, and the Sacred Tree cord. The last of these is composed of the three mystery cords entwined together, and is regarded as a single cord.

In the previous chapters you encountered various pathworkings and cauldron techniques. Some of them contained the inclusion of one type of cord or another. As you become more familiar with the cords you can include your own intuitive work using one or more of them. It is my hope and intention for you to do so, because over the course of time I want you to experience more than this single volume can provide.

To better familiarize you with the cords, let us examine each one in more detail. We will begin with the serpent, which we have depicted in various chapters as a chthonic entity and messenger between the worlds. The use of this cord is very simple.

The White Serpent
The role of the serpent in cord work is to lead you into nonmaterial reality. The cord is tied with a knot on one end, which represents the

snake's head. To use the serpent you wrap the white cord around your right wrist. Leave enough length to be able to hold the head (knot) in the skin fold area between the base of your thumb and index finger. In this fashion the snake has entwined around your wrist and is leading you head first into the inner planes. The serpent also helps to return you to material reality in the same way.

Using the white cord can enhance any Underworld or Otherworld journey. Therefore you can use it even outside of cauldron work. One example is to wear the serpent while doing oracle work such as reading cards or scrying. Wearing it during the time of Samhain can enhance contact with spirits of the dead. You can carry the serpent cord when dealing with trapped spirits in haunted areas, and help them to move on. To do this you visualize an etheric counterpart of the white serpent and pass it to them with the directive that the serpent will lead them into the Afterlife.

The Spirit Cord

In addition to the white cord you also possess the spirit cord. This cord symbolizes the "spirit mind" and projects it into nonmaterial reality. It is not used as often as the other cords because it carries your life essence with it whenever it is directed outward. Its primary use is as a shamanic tool that extends your mind and spirit body into any inner plane you want to enter. Stories about shamans retrieving lost souls are tales about traveling with such a cord.

Prior to any journey, there are two steps required to activate or vitalize the spirit cord. The cord is first coiled into a spiral, then pressed into the palm of the right hand and then into the left palm. This passes the alignment of "outward action" (right hand) with "inward receptivity" (left hand) into the cord. What passes into the cord awakens in the spirit or soul.

The next step is to breathe the *breath of life* into the cord. To do this, enfold the cord by pressing it between both palms. Open your hands at the area of the thumbs, enough that you can blow air onto the cord. You will then take a deep breath and slowly exhale it into the cord between your hands. As you exhale, visualize it glowing with a silvery light. Repeat this two more times, for a total of three altogether.

The last step is to coil the cord into a spiral, and then place it on the tip of your tongue. Make sure that you hold a loose end of the cord securely with your fingers. This will prevent you from accidently swallowing or choking on the cord if it moves back in your mouth. Next, close your lips and pull the end of the cord out about an inch (the rest of the cord is still on your tongue). For the rest of this technique you need to be sitting back in a chair. Do not stand during the rest of this procedure as people have been known to fall down at the end.

With the cord and end in place, focus your attention on your inner Cauldron of Regeneration. Visualize a glowing sphere of light rising from the cauldron. As you move this sphere of light up to your solar plexus, pull about one third of the length of the cord out through your lips.

Visualize the Cauldron of Abundance at your solar plexus and fill it with the silver light. Then visualize the sphere of light rising up and moving to your head area. As it does, pull another third of the cord out through your lips.

Visualize the Cauldron of Enlightenment receiving the silvery light into itself. Lastly, raise the sphere from the cauldron and pull the rest of the cord out through your lips. As you do, visualize the sphere of light passing out with it.

Prior to performing this technique, you need to have a destination in mind. For inner planes work, you will need to think about where you want to project your consciousness and what you want to accomplish there. The places you journeyed to during pathworking sessions are the ones you should stick to until you are more experienced with projection through the spirit cord. Use the image of the Moon Tree (Dream Gate) to pass out through, and then recall the imagery of the realm you want to enter.

For healing purposes you can project into the body of a person and attempt to remove the illness or fix the injury. You use the same process with the exception that once the cord is free from your mouth, you drop it on the part of the body you select as an entry point. Entry points should always be exactly where the problem resides. If the problem is systemic, then you should enter through the navel.

You should not have a problem returning from the inner planes journey or from healing inside a body. However, if you do have difficulty, then perform the following. Fold your hands over your navel. Imagine that a cord extends from the inner plane zone or healing area back to your body. Try to sense it and *feel* it. All that remains is to climb up the cord. As you climb, hold the image of your body sitting in the chair. This is your final destination.

If you are working with healing someone, there are a few things you need to know. Always inform yourself about the part of the body you will work on. Look at pictures in a medical book, view x-rays or MRI images, whatever it takes so that you know exactly what will appear at the end of your destination.

Once you have projected into the body, visualize the problem area and you will be there instantly. You should visualize diseased areas as dark globs. Remove them and visualize stuffing them into a plastic bag that you produce. See and remove seven blobs each time you perform a work of healing. If you are repairing an injury, visualize the bone or organ as being made of clay. Join areas together that need to mend and smooth the connection so that it looks complete. In short, look at the problem and perform a task that reverses or erases the damage.

Upon returning, it is vital that you cleanse yourself. I recommend using the bathing cauldron technique that appeared earlier in this chapter. It is important to remember that energy tends to adhere itself to anything in its immediate vicinity, and any intimate contact with the energy of disease or injury will cling to your aura. Therefore it is vital that it be removed through cleansing and purification.

The Sacred Tree Cord

This is the supreme tool of the Cauldron Keeper. As mentioned in a previous chapter, the Tree is comprised of three colored cords: red, white, and black. The traditional assignment of these colors connects them to the inner mysteries of birth, life, and death. These reflect the timeless questions: Where did we come from, why are we here, and what happens after this is done?

As a tool, the Tree joins us to the ancient and foundational concept of the Universe as once conceived of by our ancestors. This is the idea of a World Tree that represents the universe or ways of accessing levels of that Universe. In this regard, the Sacred Tree cord represents the mystical universe and the realms that compose it. It then offers a means of interfacing with each level. From there it allows us to find doorways that open into the inner planes.

The Tree can be used to call spirits from nonmaterial reality, and it can also serve to direct spirits that appear in the material realm. One very old belief is that spirits dwell in the air and move with the wind. In this context, the cord can be wielded to evoke and dismiss through the element of air.

Begin by selecting the top knot for calling Overworld spirits or the bottom knot for Underworld spirits. Hold the Tree in the commencement posture and say:

By the power of the Sacred Tree, by the power of the Triformis Goddess who holds power over the Three Worlds, I open the portal between the worlds.

Slide your hand from left to right in the manner of pushing a curtain to the side. Then activate the knot that corresponds to the spirit world you are opening, and say:

I call to you, spirits of the [Overworld/Underworld], hear my words and be favorable to me this day. In the name of the Triple Goddess who rules all worlds, I summon, stir, and call you forth.

Begin whirling the Tree cord rapidly in a clockwise manner (holding the Overworld knot if working with that realm, or the end of the three long strands if working with the Underworld). Swing the cord around fast enough to produce a whirling sound, and keep this up for a few moments as you visualize spheres of blue light gathering in front of you.

When you are ready to stop swinging, slow the motion down until the cords come to rest. Then move your fingers on the Tree to the directing position in order to keep the spirits in harmony with the intended work.

Spirits can be called to assist in various ways. Spirits from the Underworld can be called for oracle purposes and to find things that are hidden or secret. Direct them by making specific requests and then ask them to present the answers to you in your dreams. When you go to bed at night, make the affirmation that you will speak with these spirits and you will fully remember the dream session.

Spirits of the Overworld can be called for aid in understanding the mysteries, interpreting visions, receiving teachings, and for protection. Direct them by being specific about your requests. Ask to receive enlightenment during your sleep periods.

In the magical system of the cauldron, what is called in must also be returned. Using the technique of whirling the cord, you simply reverse direction and move it counterclockwise. These are the words of releasing or returning:

> I call to you, spirits of the [Overworld/Underworld], hear my words and be favorable to me this day. In the name of the Triple Goddess who rules all worlds, I summon, stir, and call you to assemble. It is time now to return to your realm and so I bid you farewell.

Visualize all the blue spheres gathered together, and then mentally picture them departing until they disappear altogether. Then bring the cord to a stop, raise it above your head, say, "By all the names of the Triformis Goddess, so be it done," and then thrust the cord forward as though you are slinging an object off into the distance. You can now put the cord away.

The Sacred Tree Cords and Prayer

The symbolism and power of the number three holds great meaning for the Cauldron Keeper. Therefore the idea of a triformis nature extends into the Cauldron Keeper's view of deity. In this light we find the concept of a triple goddess in our system.

As noted in an earlier chapter, the three short end cords represent a divine triformis feminine deity. You can use any goddess names that appeal to you, or you can simply use the term "Triple Goddess." In this section we will use the latter. The following is a simple prayer of alignment and blessing. Feel free to create your own.

Begin preparation by setting your cauldron as the centerpiece for your altar. Behind the cauldron place three candles: one red, one black, one white. You can place offerings on the altar along with flowers and other things of your choice.

Next, hold the cord upright, and then fold your hands around the Tree so that only the top knot (with the three short ends) is showing. In any classic "praying hands" formation you can make this section of the Tree protrude upward from inside your joined hands. Try a couple of arrangements and see which one works best for you.

With the three short ends in plain view, you are now ready to say the prayer:

I call to the Triformis Goddess, you who holds the power of birth, life and death and who rules the Three Great Worlds. Hear my words and be favorable to me this day. I ask for your blessings, which bring to my life gain over loss, growth over decline, union over isolation, and strength over weakness.

Now touch the ends of the cord to your body in the following order and say:

- Forehead: "I *receive the blessings of the Goddess in my mind.*"
- Genitals: "I *receive the blessings of the Goddess in my body.*"
- Chest: "I *receive the blessings of the Goddess in my spirit.*"

In the inner mystery tradition, we also find the *Three Daughters of Necessity*. These are the legendary Three Fates who weave the patterns of our lives. However, in the mystery tradition it is not taught that human life is predestined and that we just run the preconstructed maze until we drop.

The mystery tradition holds that we inspire the Fates to weave the patterns of our lives from the energy of the choices we make and the character we bring to our lives and the lives of those we touch. It is further taught that the time of our death changes as the patterns emerge. In other words, death may have approached us at several key junctions in our lives, but was inspired to move on to await another day.

A prayer using the cords is to the Daughters of Necessity. Set your cauldron on your altar space. As an offering, set a spool of thread with a pair of scissors in front of the cauldron. You can add flowers and other items as you feel moved to do so.

When you are ready to pray, interlace your fingers and bring the palms together to form "praying hands." The knot representing the Overworld is positioned to protrude up between your crossed thumbs. If done correctly you will only see the top knot and the three short ends jetting out from the top of your hands. Next, move the Tree so that the long ends of the cord are at navel level. You are now ready to say the prayer:

I call to the Daughters of Necessity to hear my words and be favorable to me this day. I ask that you weave for me all that is best in life: love, health, prosperity, well-being, happiness, and good fortune. Klotho, please spin a thread of great beauty. Lakhesis, please extend further the work at hand. Atropos, please be patient awhile longer and stay your hand.

You can also say this prayer on behalf of someone else. If the person is gravely ill you can hold the Tree over that person's navel during the prayer (and of course you will insert his or her name into the wording of the prayer).

Daily Alignment

The Cauldron Keeper incorporates her or his spirituality into all facets of life, whether the time is preparing for a festival celebration or simply getting ready to go to work each day. Because the keeper operates within all worlds, she or he knows there is no separation, and that any differences are due to perception.

The goal of the keeper is to maintain an inner balance. This requires establishing the "center of being" before engaging the world and all who inhabit it (whether we are talking about material reality or nonmaterial reality). To accomplish this task, the Sacred Tree cords are used as a focal point for spiritual alignment.

Begin each day with the following routine (or customize it to suit your needs). Hold the Tree upright with the right hand while squeezing the three short ends of the cords between the thumb and index finger. Holding firmly, take your left hand and grasp the large top knot representing the Overworld with your thumb and index finger. Say the following words as you slide the fingers of your left hand down to the knots at the bottom of the long strands:

As above, so below, as within, so without, as the many, so the one.

Now, pass the section with the three large knots over to the left palm. Cup both hands together so that you are cradling the three knots. Proceed now with the following set of steps:

- Raise the Tree upward and say, "*I ask for and receive blessings from the realm above. My thoughts this day will generate and attract a more enlightened view.*"
- Lower the Tree downward and say, "*I ask for and receive blessings from below. My thoughts this day will generate and attract a firmer foundation for all I create.*"
- Present the Tree to the east quarter and say, "*I ask for and receive the blessings of elemental air. My thoughts this day will generate and attract prosperity, health, peace, and wellbeing.*"
- Present the Tree to the south quarter and say, "*I ask for and receive the blessings of elemental fire. My passion this day will generate and attract changes that initiate prosperity, health, peace, and well-being.*"

- Present the Tree to the west quarter and say, "*I ask for and receive the blessings of elemental water. My feelings this day will generate and attract prosperity, health, peace, and well-being.*"
- Present the Tree to the north quarter and say, "*I ask for and receive the blessings of elemental earth. My presence this day will generate and attract prosperity, health, peace, and well-being.*"

At this stage you are prepared to go about your day under the influence of a high spiritual vibration. Try and nurture this quality throughout the day. People and situations will certainly present challenges to maintaining your inner balance. Spirituality within material reality is never an easy path. If it were easy, then it would become mundane, which in turn would remove its distinction. The spiritual path is a noble one because it is challenging and calls upon us to rise to our higher nature.

FOURTEEN

FAREWELL AT THE CROSSROADS

•

Now that we have arrived at the end of this book, it will be beneficial to look back on our journey. In doing so, we can better understand how everything comes together into one picture. It is through seeing the connections and integrating various elements that our comprehension is enriched.

Throughout this book we have looked at the inner mysteries of the cauldron. At the core is the idea of regeneration. The concept of regeneration took us through teachings of transformation and renewal. These foundational elements serve to break down the barriers that prevent us from recovering the forgotten past. They also inspire us to believe in the limitless, if not the impossible.

The Cauldron Keeper lives with a sense that material reality is only part of a greater existence, and that recorded history is often the political rendering of the victors. As we have seen, the keeper is inspired by ancient cauldron tales of the Quest, and in these he or she hears the message that our knowledge and wisdom are incomplete. There are things that are hidden, veiled, or entirely lost. The keeper knows there is more to history than the views of those who prevailed; there is also the unspoken story of those who were vanquished.

Because the keeper believes in nonmaterial reality, he or she looks there for additional perspective and for messages of the past. In previous chapters we have noted the belief that spirits of the dead were called upon for oracle. This reminds us of the belief that the dead know things the living cannot. Herein is the clue that nonmaterial reality plays a vital role in material reality. Unfortunately this is often ignored or dismissed in contemporary society, but this was not always the case, as we know that cultures of the past venerated the ancestors as a surviving and interacting consciousness. The Roman concept of the Lare is but one example.

In addition to ancestral spirits, the Cauldron Keeper believes in a consciousness of the earth that is called the *spirit of the land*. A similar belief is found in many primitive cultures and also appears in American Indian beliefs where the earth is referred to as the Mother. For the keeper, the earth itself is the Great Cauldron from which terrestrial life issues forth and returns again in the endless cycles of birth, life, death, and rebirth.

One of the classic beliefs in occult theory is the existence of the Akashic Records. This is often described as a spiritual library on the inner planes wherein everything that has ever transpired on the earth is recorded. The Cauldron Keeper sees this concept more simply, regarding it as the living memory of the earth itself.

Earlier in the book we encountered the idea of the teachings of oak and boulder. The ancient Greek writer Hesiod refers to them is his *Theogony* and surmises them to be teachings that pre-exist civilized culture. In an esoteric sense, we can view the teachings of oak and boulder as the passing on of living memory. This evokes the image of rock, as the spirit of the land, passing memory to the oak whereby it is kept within a living entity. Such a view adds another dimension to the ancient practice of establishing sacred groves and venerating trees. This was a widespread practice among our ancestors.

Author James Frazer, in his book *The Golden Bough* (1928), mentions the old belief that spirits of the dead reside in trees. In another of his works, *The Belief in Immortality and the Worship of the Dead* (1913), Frazer states that spirits of the dead await rebirth inside a tree. This may be at the core of the old folk custom of splitting a sapling and passing a newborn baby through its opening.

Occultist Lewis Spence, in his book *Encyclopedia of Occultism and Parapsychology* (1960), writes:

There was a strange sympathy between trees and mankind, and great honour was paid to the sacred trees of Rome. On the oak tree of Jupiter the triumphant general hung the shield and arms of his fallen foe; while the hedges about the Temple of Diana at Nemi were covered with votive offerings. The trees also harboured the spirits of the dead who came forth as dreams to the souls of men.

Spence's words reflect the idea that our ancestors speak to us in the dream state. This is a concept that I have included in several chapters, and one that is key to cauldron work. The dream state is one of the inner planes of nonmaterial reality where messages are received and interpreted.

As we have seen, the cauldron system uses three levels of consciousness that are objectified as vessels. It is through them that we can examine and interpret ancestral messages and memories. The keeper draws upon a higher consciousness to oversee this process, and in the chapters of our book this consciousness is personified in deity form as the god Hermes. As a messenger god who interprets foreign communication, there is perhaps no better connection for us in this work.

Throughout this book, our work was not only with gods, myths, and legends, but also with energy, metaphysics, and the new biological science of morphogenetics. It is important for the Cauldron Keeper to achieve a balance between material reality and nonmaterial reality, lest one overpower the other. To lose balance is to collapse portals, which leaves the keeper solidly in one realm versus the other. When such a state arises we have, in effect, lost the cauldron or failed to return it.

The underlying theme throughout our book has been based on the ancient Bardic tales of lost cauldrons. Our focus has been on the need to embark on a sacred Quest to retrieve that which is lost. We saw this theme as a metaphor for the spiritual condition and as a prophecy that holds the key for future generations. This key opens doorways to the past, and back to a time when humankind lived in *common cause* with the spirit of the land.

For the keeper, the cauldron is a symbol of regeneration, renewal, and integration. The past is not lost to us because it still exists in the ancestral memory. This memory exists because it resides in the living matter of our DNA. This DNA is the living descendant surviving from an unbroken chain of donors since the beginning of our race. It is the cauldron's brew, and we are the ladle.

In practice the inner cauldrons are operational modes of consciousness where the past, present, and future intersect. The ancestral notion of the cauldron as a magical tool is a sign that this idea is part of the human psyche. Its appearance in ancient myth and legend is evidence of this and suggests a state of consciousness as much as it does a physical vessel. Here again we see the merging of material reality and nonmaterial reality dovetailing into the concept of the cauldron.

In a previous chapter of our book we looked at the symbolism of the skull and crossbones. We noted that the skull in ancient Celtic culture represented what remained of a person's life experience after his or her death. Within various cauldron tales we noted the theme of resurrecting the dead by placing their remains (often bones) in the cauldron. Herein lies the metaphor of the cauldron as the vessel of renewal, regeneration, and integration. It is within the cauldron that we manifest our ancestors and bring forth all previous states of the past.

Another tool we discovered in relationship to the theme of retrieval is the cord. We came to know the cords as conveyors of consciousness and also as extensions of ourselves into other realities. Spiritual cords are, in essence, threads of lineage. They connect and entwine, draw and retrieve, hold and suspend. Through them every person can claim his or her heredity.

As we neared the end of the book we arrived at the hearth. We noted that the hearth was the center of the home, and represented the place from which both physical and spiritual nourishment was supplied. In his book *Folklore by the Fireside* (1980), anthropologist Alessandro Falassi discusses the old-world family traditions associated with the hearth. One of the main themes is the tradition of passing on stories of family lineage. Each generation hears the historical accounts of its ancestors as told by a designated keeper of tradition.

An important element in Falassi's book is the mention of tree symbolism. The tree has been an important part of the cauldron retrieval work. Falassi mentions a specific ceremony that was observed in front of the hearth. The observation required selecting a log cut from the portion of the tree trunk closest to the roots. This clearly indicates the importance of rootedness in the ceremony.

Falassi notes the ancient Roman tradition of incorporating a log into the marriage ritual and the custom of referring to the woman as the tree of life. He also notes that the hearth kettle (cauldron) was viewed as a feminine symbol. In various chapters of our book we encountered the theme of the tree possessing a Faery Door in its trunk, which resembles female genitalia. We also looked at the principle of impregnating the cauldron with formed thoughts. In both of these we see a strong connection to the feminine as the "womb gate," through which spirit enters into the material world and manifests as a result. It is how thoughts become things.

The hearth is a powerful symbol for the Cauldron Keeper. It is not only where the sacred divine fire burns, but is also the abode of the cauldron itself, and in this sense it is the Temple of the Cauldron. As a symbol, the hearth reminds the keeper that he or she is the guardian of tradition. As a guardian, the keeper knows that tradition must be a living thing and a flowing process. It must adapt to new environments and yet ever remain true to itself.

The fire in the center of the hearth is never domesticated, even though humans may have regarded it as such. It is only the hearth itself that represents domestication. The fire, as the divine flame, is unchanging. It is truth that cannot be distorted, for nothing can change the nature of fire. It is human nature that can and must change in the light of the fireplace. This is why fire is a symbol of transformation.

The image of the cauldron suspended over the hearth fire is, for the keeper, a symbol of spiritual and magical transformation. In this regard the cauldron is the material existence: fixed, limited, and constant. The fire is the divine force that boils and churns the contents of the cauldron. We can call this the fire of inspiration. The steam rising from the cauldron is the spiritual quintessence—the pure, highly concentrated essence of a thing. It is part fire, brew, cauldron, and vapor.

In ancient and medieval philosophy the concept of quintessence was defined as the fifth element, a higher nature than the four creative elements of earth, air, fire, and water. Ancient thought held that the fifth element was the light of the celestial bodies, a property latent in all things.

It is noteworthy that the word quintessence is derived from the Latin *quinta*, a feminine rendering of the number five, and *essentia*, which means "essence." In ancient times fire was considered a feminine element (Hestia/Vesta/Brigit) and it is through the female that the essence of man and woman is transformed into new life. The Cauldron Keeper uses the feminine forces of the cauldron and transformation to manifest the regeneration of ancestral memory, which is in effect a new life from an old life.

As is often the case when we step into the mystical, we arrive now at the crossroads, the in-between place. This book has provided the basic tools and vital concepts to practice the cauldron system. You can experiment with this and use elements adapted to what you already practice and believe. The choice of whether to become a Cauldron Keeper is also before you. To take on this role is to guard and protect tradition, while at the same time work to assure its ongoing survival.

In closing, may Trivia, the goddess of all roads, shed her light upon the choices ahead in the path you walk. May Hermes, the god of travel and the escort of the spirits of the dead, be a faithful companion at your side. In bidding you farewell, I end with the blessings of the Cauldron Keeper:

May your hearth fire burn bright in the night, and your visions be guided by light.

BIBLIOGRAPHY

Alexiou, Margaret. *The Ritual Lament in Greek Tradition*. London: Cambridge University Press, 1974.

Ashcroft-Nowicki, Dolores. *Highways of the Mind*. Wellingborough, UK: Aquarian Press, 1987.

Campbell, Joseph. *Primitive Mythology*. New York: Akana, 1991.

Dorman, Rushton M. *The Origin of Primitive Superstitions*. Philadelphia: J. B. Lippincott & Co., 1881.

Falassi, Alessandro. *Folklore by the Fireside*. Austin, TX: University of Texas Press, 1980.

Foxwood, Orion. *The Tree of Enchantment: Ancient Wisdom and Magical Practice of the Faery Tradition*. San Francisco: Red Wheel/Weiser, 2008.

Frazer, James George. *The Belief in Immortality and the Worship of the Dead*. London: MacMillan and Co., 1913.

———. *The Golden Bough*. New York: The MacMillan Company, 1928.

Gummere, Francis B. *Old English Ballads*. Boston: Ginn & Company, Publishers, 1897.

Hastings, John. *Encyclopaedia of Religion and Ethics*, Vol. VIII. New York: Charles Scribner's Sons, 1916.

Head, Joseph, and S. L. Carson. *Reincarnation: An East-West Anthology*. Mamaroneck, NY: Aeon Publishing Company, 2000.

Henderson, Joseph, and Maud Oakes. *The Wisdom of the Serpent: The Myths of Death, Rebirth, and Resurrection*. Princeton, NJ: Princeton University Press, 1990.

Herbert, Algernon. *Britannia After the Romans*. London: Henry G. Bohn, 1836.

Lethaby, William Richard. *Architecture, Mysticism and Myth: Sacred Geometry*. Charleston, SC: Forgotten Books, 2007.

MacEowen, Frank. *The Spiral of Memory and Belonging: A Celtic Path of Soul and Kinship*. Novato, CA: New World Library, 2004.

Manciocco, Claudia, and Luigi Manciocco. *Una Casa Senza Porte: Viaggio intorno all figura della Befana*. Rome: Melusina, 1995.

Massey, Gerald. *Ancient Egypt: The Light of the World*. London: T. Fisher Unwin, 1907.

Matthews, John, and Caitlín Matthews. *Walkers Between the Worlds*. Rochester, VT: Inner Traditions, 2003.

Miller, Jeffrey C. *The Transcendent Function: Jung's Model of Psychological Growth through Dialogue with the Unconscious*. New York: State University of New York Press, 2004.

Mulford, Prentice. *Thoughts Are Things*. New York: Barnes & Noble, 2007.

Narby, Jeremy. *The Cosmic Serpent: DNA and the Origins of Knowledge*. New York: Putnam, 1998.

Sagan, Carl. *Shadows of Forgotten Ancestors*. New York: Ballantine, 1992.

Sheldrake, Rupert. *A New Science of Life*. Rochester, VT: Park Street Press, 1995.

————. *The Presence of the Past: Morphic Resonance & the Habits of Nature*. Rochester, VT: Park Street Press, 1995.

Song, Tamarack. *Journey to the Ancestral Self*. Barrytown, NY: Station Hill Press, 1994.

Spence, Lewis. *Encyclopedia of Occultism and Parapsychology*. New York: University Books, 1960.

Varner, Gary. *Menhirs, Dolmen, and Circles of Stone: The Folklore and Magic of Sacred Stone*. New York: Algora Publishing, 2004.

INDEX

To Write to the Author

If you wish to contact the author or would like more information about this book, please write to the author in care of Llewellyn Worldwide and we will forward your request. Both the author and publisher appreciate hearing from you and learning of your enjoyment of this book and how it has helped you. Llewellyn Worldwide cannot guarantee that every letter written to the author can be answered, but all will be forwarded. Please write to:

Raven Grimassi
℅ Llewellyn Worldwide
2143 Wooddale Drive, Dept. 978-0-7387-1575-9
Woodbury, MN 55125-2989, U.S.A.
Please enclose a self-addressed stamped envelope for reply,
or $1.00 to cover costs. If outside U.S.A., enclose
international postal reply coupon.

Many of Llewellyn's authors have websites with additional information and resources. For more information, please visit our website at http://www.llewellyn.com

Free Catalog

Get the latest information on our body, mind, and spirit products! To receive a **free** copy of Llewellyn's consumer catalog, *New Worlds of Mind & Spirit,* simply call 1-877-NEW-WRLD or visit our website at www.llewellyn.com and click on *New Worlds.*

LLEWELLYN ORDERING INFORMATION

Order Online:
Visit our website at www.llewellyn.com, select your books, and order them on our secure server.

Order by Phone:
- Call toll-free within the U.S. at 1-877-NEW-WRLD (1-877-639-9753). Call toll-free within Canada at 1-866-NEW-WRLD (1-866-639-9753)
- We accept VISA, MasterCard, and American Express

Order by Mail:
Send the full price of your order (MN residents add 6.875% sales tax) in U.S. funds, plus postage & handling to:

> **Llewellyn Worldwide**
> **2143 Wooddale Drive, Dept. 978-0-7387-1575-9**
> **Woodbury, MN 55125-2989**

Postage & Handling:

Standard (U.S., Mexico, & Canada). If your order is:
> $24.99 and under, add $4.00
> $25.00 and over, FREE STANDARD SHIPPING

AK, HI, PR: $16.00 for one book plus $2.00 for each additional book.

International Orders (airmail only):
> $16.00 for one book plus $3.00 for each additional book

Orders are processed within 2 business days.
Please allow for normal shipping time. Postage and handling rates subject to change.

The Well Worn Path

Raven Grimassi and Stephanie Taylor

Art by Mickie Mueller

The Well Worn Path is much more than a divination tool. Specifically designed for Witches, Wiccans, and Pagans, this uniquely Pagan system is based on the roots of Pagan culture and practice.

Depicting symbolism and imagery vital to nature-based spirituality, the multifaceted, forty-card deck can be used for learning, teaching, ritual, and personal alignment. Each card has an assigned meaning, teaching element, and meditation for spiritual alignment that, altogether, communicates a vital Pagan concept or tenet. It's a magical, transforming journey for students or teachers seeking to understand the hidden Mysteries and embrace the Old Ways.

978-0-7387-0671-9, Boxed kit includes 40-card deck, 216-pp. book, and organdy bag $22.95

The Hidden Path

Raven Grimassi and Stephanie Taylor

Art by Mickie Mueller

Raven Grimassi and Stephanie Taylor—creators of *The Well Worn Path*—introduce another innovative system exclusively for Pagans, Witches, and Wiccans.

Steeped in Pagan tradition, practice, and symbolism, *The Hidden Path* guides you to the tenets of this nature-based spirituality. Sensuous, vivid artwork captures the Sabbats, the Fates, Karma, Centers of Power, the Great Rite, and other Pagan practices and beliefs still relevant today. Use this multi-faceted tool for celebrating seasonal rites, creating ritual experiences, pathworking, and accessing the hidden Mysteries of the Craft. You'll also find a story woven throughout the deck for creating mystical alignments between you and the spiritual keys in the card imagery. The enclosed guidebook features interpretations and keywords of each card, divination spreads, and suggestions for incorporating the cards into your Sabbat celebrations.

978-0-7387-1070-9, Boxed kit includes 40-card deck, 216-pp. book,
     and organdy bag $19.95

Spirit of the Witch

Religion & Spirituality in Contemporary Witchcraft

RAVEN GRIMASSI

Find peace and happiness in the spiritual teachings of the Craft.

What is in the spirit of the Witch? What empowers Witches in their daily and spiritual lives? How does a person become a Witch?

In *Spirit of the Witch*, Raven Grimassi, an initiate of several Wiccan traditions, reveals the Witch as a citizen living and working like all others—and as a spiritual being who seeks alignment with the natural world. He provides an overview of the Witch's view of deity and how it manifests in the cycles of nature. Seasonal rituals, tools, magic, and beliefs are all addressed in view of their spiritual underpinnings. Additionally, he shows the relationship among elements of pre-Christian European religion and modern Witchcraft beliefs, customs, and practices.

978-0-7387-0338-1, 264 pp., 6 x 9 $12.95

Wiccan Magick

Inner Teachings of the Craft

RAVEN GRIMASSI

Wiccan Magick is a serious and complete study for those who desire to understand the inner meanings, techniques, and symbolism of magick as an occult art. Magick within modern Wicca is an eclectic blending of many occult traditions that evolved from the ancient beliefs and practices in both Europe, the Middle East, and Asia. *Wiccan Magick* covers the full range of magickal and ritual practices as they pertain to both modern ceremonial and shamanic Wicca.

Come to understand the evolution of the Craft, the ancient magickal current that flows from the past to the present, and the various aspects included in ritual, spellcasting, and general theology. When you understand why something exists within a ritual structure, you will know better how to build upon the underlying concepts to create ritual that is meaningful to you.

978-1-56718-255-2, 264 pp., 6 x 9 $14.95

To order, call 1-877-NEW-WRLD
Prices subject to change without notice
Order at Llewellyn.com 24 hours a day, 7 days a week!

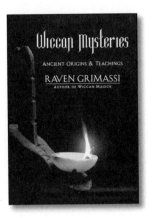

The Wiccan Mysteries
Ancient Origins & Teachings
RAVEN GRIMASSI

Once reserved for a select few, the initiate-level teachings of Wicca are revealed in this award-winning guide. Daring and honest, *The Wiccan Mysteries* is a must-have complement to your personal practice.

Author Raven Grimassi takes you on a comprehensive tour of Wicca—its pre-Christian historical and theological roots in Old Europe and continuing through to modern America. These multicultural origins form the basis for contemporary Wicca and empower it as a dynamic system for spiritual development.

Uncover the hidden meanings of sacred writings and explore the major tenets of the Craft—from reincarnation, the God and Goddess, magickal arts, and planes of existence to symbols, rites, and ethics. Learn how to create an astral temple, consecrate ritual tools, and work with magickal familiars.

978-1-56718-254-5, 312 pp., 6 x 9 $16.95